OPPORTUNITIES FOR STUDENT DEVELOPMENT IN TWO-YEAR COLLEGES

Edited By

Don G. Creamer
Associate Professor
College of Education
Virginia Tech

Charles R. Dassance
Vice President of Student Affairs
Florida Junior College at Jacksonville

Volume 6; NASPA Monograph Series
Published by the National Association
of Student Personnel Administrators, Inc.

I

Library of Congress Cataloging-in-Publication Data
Opportunities for student development in two-year colleges.
 (NASPA monograph series ; v. 6)
 Includes bibliographies.
 1. College student development programs—United States. 2.
Junior colleges—United States. I. Creamer, Don G., 1936-. II.
Dassance, Charles R., 1945-   . III. National Association of
Student Personnel Administrators (U.S.) IV. Series.
LB2343.4.066 1986   378'.1543   86-23716
ISBN 0-931654-08-4

NASPA Monograph Board 1985-86

NASPA Monograph Board 1986-87

Volume 6 Edited by 1985-86 and 1986-87 Monograph Boards

SOCIAL SCIENCE & HISTORY DIVISION
EDUCATION & PHILOSOPHY SECTION

Contents

Page

Foreword V

Chapter 1:
Opportunities in Legacy 1
  Charles R. Dassance

Chapter 2:
Opportunities in Diversity 21
  Steven R. Helfgot

Chapter 3:
Opportunities Through Interdependence 37
  Edward W. Phoenix, R. Thomas Flynn,
  Deborah L. Floyd

Chapter 4:
Opportunities in Challenge 55
  John Cordova, Kay Martens

Chapter 5:
Opportunities in the Future 73
  Don G. Creamer

Foreword

Intentionally promoting students' development is problematic under the best of circumstances. Evidence suggests, however, that development during the college years may be associated with intentional, programmatic efforts by student affairs professionals. Though it is impossible to partition the effects related to professional efforts from effects related to natural occurrences and maturity, demonstrable effects on student development do occur and stand as a tribute to the quality of professional service in higher education.

The major ingredients of a developmental environment— that is, one that promotes growth and change in participants— appears to include at least the following: the simultaneous presence of forces that *challenge* the participant and forces that *support* the participant (Sanford, 1966), *time* to allow for multiple interactions with people and with events (Astin, 1977), *involvement* of participants in opportunities for learning (Astin, 1984), and *effort* by the participant (Pace, 1984). Considered as correlates of student development, these conditions generally are accepted by professionals in college student affairs as corequisites of effective student development programming. Yet none of these conditions or correlates offer equal potential for stimulating student development in the two-year college as in the four-year college, either by natural occurrence or by intentional intervention. The circumstances of short time duration, commuter status of students, part-time enrollment patterns, the dominance of a career-oriented curriculum, and infrequent opportunity for student/faculty or student/student interaction create unequal opportunity for promoting development in the two-year college.

Both an ethical dilemma and a professional challenge for two-year college student affairs professionals arise from this condition. The ethical dilemma is rooted in a *knowledge* of unequal results in promoting student development when compared to four-year college efforts (Astin, 1977) existing coterminously with the *reality* that two-year student affairs programs generally mirror four-year college operations. Different and better service to two-year college students is needed, but little evidence exists that improvements are imminent. The challenge for professionals lies in the two-year college historical commitment to student-oriented services and its juxtaposition with current systemic problems that cry out for creative solution.

This monograph, addressed primarily to the concerns of practitioners, was written for the most part by two-year college practitioners. The editors charged the authors to present an analysis of *opportunities* for promoting student development inherent in the special nature of the two-year college. Discussions of the legacy of commitment to students, the recognition of diversity of student characteristics, the requirements for interdependency vis-à-vis other agencies and institutions, the knowledge of environmental effects on students, and future possibilities provided the structure for each chapter. Each discussion is summarized by noting specific *challenges* for professionals.

The two-year college rivals the land-grant university in terms of its contribution to the American pluralistic system of higher education. Its special contributions include opening new markets for learners both by offering curricula tailored to community need and by extending its offerings to all adult citizens of the community regardless of prior educational experience. These qualities of the two-year college as well as its special commitment to guidance of students and to teaching as a primary thrust of educational service are discussed by Dassance in Chapter 1. He underscores the uneven results of student affairs practice during the 20th century and challenges the profession to be more responsive to factual legacy.

The heterogeneous characteristics of the typical two-year college student are well-documented in literature. In Chapter 2, Helfgot uses this richness of client talent to demonstrate how special the two-year college is for practicing student affairs. His portrait of two-year college students appears as a collage and stands as vivid testimony of the inadequacies inherent in conventional practices—that is, practices normally associated with four-year colleges—when applied in the two-year college environment.

One of the truly distinctive characteristics of the two-year college is its reliance for success on interdependent relationships with other institutions or segments of society. Its relationship to four-year colleges and universities is well known; however, other relationships, especially within the community surrounding the college, serve equally to determine each college's destiny. Chapter 3 contains an analysis of the opportunities in these interdependent relationships by Phoenix, Flynn, and Floyd that stands as a unique contribution to the literature of the field. A powerful challenge to maximize these opportunities is offered that reflects a rare insight into the extraordinary roles of student affairs professionals.

The heart of the dilemma introduced earlier—forces associated with promoting student development in four-year colleges and universities simply do not have the same consequences in two-year institutions—is addressed by Cordova and Martens in Chapter 4. An incisive analysis of the real consequences on student development of certain mediating forces also is offered. Cordova and Martens visualize many opportunities for leadership in the profession, especially in organizations outside the community college.

Opportunities for student development are addressed in Chapter 5. Creamer describes and analyzes certain characteristics of a potent learning environment, a proposed standard of organization effectiveness for the profession, and a profile of the new leader needed in the two-year college. He calls for better service to a more demanding clientele than is typically provided in other types of colleges and universities and suggests that the source of advice for more adequate service lies with researchers, historians, and philosophers rather than with practitioners, institutional administrators, or other educational leaders. Certain principles for practice are suggested as a summary to guide the practitioner in the two-year college.

References

Astin, A. W. (1984). Student involvement: A developmental theory for higher education. *Journal of College Student Personnel, 25,* 297-308.

Astin, A. W. (1977). *Four critical years.* San Francisco: Jossey-Bass.

Pace, C. R. (1984). *Measuring the quality of college student experiences.* Los Angeles: Higher Education Research Institute, Graduate School of Education, UCLA.

Sanford, N. (1966). *Self and society.* New York: Atherton.

AUTHORS

John Cordova is Provost of the Northeast Valley Education Center of Maricopa Community Colleges in Phoenix (AZ).

Don G. Creamer is Associate Professor in the College of Education at Virginia Tech in Blacksburg (VA).

Charles R. Dassance is Vice President of Student Affairs at Florida Junior College in Jacksonville (FL).

Deborah L. Floyd is Vice President for Student Development at Collin County Community College District in McKinney (TX).

Thomas Flynn is Vice President for Student Affairs at Monroe Community College in Rochester (NY).

Steven Helfgot is Acting Vice President for Student Development at Oakton Community College in Des Plaines (IL).

Kay Martens is Vice Provost at Northeast Valley Education Center of Maricopa Community Colleges in Phoenix (AZ).

Edward Phoenix is Assistant Vice President for Student Affairs at Monroe Community College in Rochester (NY).

Chapter 1

Opportunities in Legacy

Charles R. Dassance

The majority of students entering college today enroll at a two-year college. It is remarkable that such a statement can be made about a segment of American postsecondary education that, for all practical purposes, did not exist before the turn of the 20th century.

In 1984-85, there were 1,221 two-year colleges in the United States enrolling 4,836,819 students (Staff, 1985). An obvious societal commitment has been made to two-year colleges, a commitment based, in part, on society's desire to expand postsecondary education opportunities to those who previously lacked opportunities and who desired to improve their personal options through participation in postsecondary education.

The purposes of this chapter are to trace the historical evolution of the two-year college and the roles of student affairs within them to promote student development. This chapter is also used to set the stage for the essays that follow.

The "Opportunity College" in Perspective

There is no typical two-year college anymore than there is a typical four-year college. Considerable diversity in the size, institutional type, and mission of two-year colleges is common. Per-

1

haps the most appropriate definition for a two-year college is the one offered by Cohen and Brawer (1982): "any institution accredited to award the associate in arts or sciences as its highest degree" (pp. 5-6). This is a very broad definition, but breadth is a requirement to accommodate the institutional diversity of two-year colleges.

It is possible to use the theme of opportunity as the thread that connects the historical roots of the two-year college. Monroe (1972) makes a clear case for the theoretical foundations of the two-year college coming from those same principles that guided public school education in America: (a) universal opportunity for a free public education for all persons, (b) local control, and (c) relevant curriculum designed to meet the needs of the individual and the nation. One of the significant roots of the two-year college in America is the public secondary school, and the tradition of opportunity that promoted public school education is the same one that supported the evolution of the two-year college.

Probably the most significant historical factor in laying the groundwork for expanding higher educational opportunities was the 1862 Morrill Act. This act clearly established an expanded and more utilitarian direction for American higher education and contributed greatly to what Vaughan (1982) refers to as the "democratized theme" of the two-year college. The Morrill Act expanded opportunities for low-cost college education for common people, firmly established the principle of federal support for education, and expanded the curriculum to more practical concerns (Monroe, 1972). The two-year college combined these principles with those that guided the public secondary schools to create educational opportunities unforeseen in 1862.

While there were a few private, postsecondary, two-year schools operating in the mid-1800s, it was not until the latter part of the nineteenth century, and especially the early part of the twentieth century, that the actual development of the two-year college began (Medsker & Tillery, 1971). Ironically, some of America's most distinguished university educators, particularly those schooled in the tradition of the German university, cleared the way for the establishment of the two-year college. Henry P. Tappen, the president of the University of Michigan, was the first American educator to recommend the transference of the first two years of college to the secondary schools (Brick, 1964, cited in Monroe, 1972). Other prominent educators of the day, such as W. W. Falwell at the University of Minnesota, Edmund J. James at the University of Illinois, and especially William Rainey Harper at the University of Chicago, were active in promoting the concept of the "upward extension of public high schools to include college courses" (Monroe, 1972, p. 10). On the West Coast, Alexis F. Lange, dean of the School of Education of the University of California, and David Starr Jordan, president of Leland Stanford Junior University, were promoting the concept of junior colleges in California. Lange, in particular, viewed the junior college as a significant step toward the goal of universal education (Monroe, 1972), a very different impetus from that of Harper and his colleagues, who were more concerned with creating a *true* university by relegating the first two years of college to the high school level. Regardless, the concept of the junior college was established. It would only be a matter of time before the *opportunity tradition* would engulf the junior college and broaden its original mission.

The next major factor that influenced the development of the two-year college and would lead to greater opportunities for students was the development of occupational programs. The early focus of the junior college was clearly on the transfer function, influenced by university presidents who saw it as a place for students to take *general education* courses before coming to the university. For the two-year college to evolve into a comprehensive institution, a broader curriculum was required.

Thornton (1966) considers the period from 1920 to 1945 as "the expansion of occupation programs" phase in the development of the two-year college. The American Association of Community and Junior Colleges, which Vaughan (1982) considers one of the major developments in the history of two-year colleges, was formed in 1920 and, in 1922, defined the junior college as ". . . an institution offering two years of instruction of strictly collegiate grade" (Eells, 1940, cited in Thornton, 1966). Three years later, the definition was expanded by the junior college association to include the concept of occupational education (Thornton, 1966).

Medsker and Tillery (1971) credit the initiation and development of occupational programs in two-year colleges to the Smith-Hughes vocational education legislation enacted during the 1920s as a reaction to economic needs brought on by the Depression. The expansion of the curriculum to include more *utilitarian* programs was accompanied by an increase in the number of two-year colleges. In 1929, there were 403 two-year colleges but that number had grown to 584 by 1945 (Monroe, 1972).

The next 40 years (1945 to 1985) in the history of the two-year college was a time of great change and phenomenal growth. Beginning in the late 1940s, the functions of adult education and community services were added to the mission of the two-year college and, coupled with the earlier functions of transfer and occupational education, led to the common use of the term *comprehensive* community college to describe two-year colleges (Thornton, 1966). The term *community college* was first used formally in 1948 in the Report of the President's Commission on Higher Education, *Higher Education for American Democracy* (Vaughan, 1983). That report also endorsed the concept of expanding educational opportunities for students to two years beyond high school. Vaughan concluded that so strong and clear was support for community colleges and their role in democratizing higher education, that the report ". . . can indeed be viewed as the community college's manifesto" (p. 24).

This theme of broadening education opportunities continued over the next several decades. President Dwight D. Eisenhower's Committee on Education Beyond the High School, 1955-56, reiterated the focus on equal educational opportunity through grades 13 and 14, as did the National Education Association ten years later in 1964 (Monroe, 1972). Major Federal legislation enacted during the 1960s gave backbone to the equal opportunity rhetoric, including the Civil Rights Act of 1964.

Concurrent with supporting governmental reports was another significant occurrence. For the first time, in 1948, the number of public two-year colleges outnumbered private two-year colleges (Monroe, 1972). By the early 1950s, the pieces were in place for community colleges to experience rapid and significant growth well into the 1970s. By 1970, the Carnegie Committee on

Higher Education concluded that "The Community College was considered to be the best institution to provide a low-cost, tuition-free, broad-and-flexible curriculum type of college education for the majority of youth" (p. 5). Thus, with roots in the move to extend the public high schools to grades 13 and 14, with encouragement from educators schooled in the German University model, and with a broadening mission to include occupational, adult education and community services programs, the two-year college emerged as the comprehensive community college.

In order for social change to occur, both new values and economic necessity are required (Naisbitt & Aburdene, 1985). In the case of American higher education, it appears that these elements were present beginning in the late 1940s and that the community college movement was one of the resulting social changes. With increased value placed on educational opportunities for larger numbers of people, with expectations for a higher standard of living, and with a need to provide better educated workers to perform more complex tasks, the community college captured the spirit of expanded opportunity in postsecondary education. From humble beginnings near the turn of the 20th century, the community college grew into a key segment of American postsecondary education, one that enrolled 55% of all first-time freshmen in the fall term, 1982 (Staff, 1984).

It is, of course, undeniable that community colleges have been a major factor in expanding educational opportunities. Many students have entered through the *open door*, a descriptive phrase capturing both a philosophical and operational admission policy commitment. It would seem logical that the diversity in intellectual and social bounds of such students would require a comprehensive program of student services to provide various kinds of support that might be required for student success. The remainder of this chapter will focus on the historical role of student affairs services to promote development in two-year college students.

Student Affairs: A Brief History of the Profession

Just as it is inadequate to use the term *two-year college* as a definition, there is similar difficulty in describing the field of student affairs. The term with the deepest historical roots is *student personnel*, but this term is used less frequently, and there is no common agreement within the profession about what terminology should be used in its place.

For the purpose of this discussion, it is useful to define the function of student affairs broadly. Fenske (1980a) indicates that a student affairs professional is one whose main salaried responsibilities are carried out in those functional areas recognized as student-oriented services. This perspective is useful for an historical consideration of student affairs functions in the two-year college, as it permits consideration of various terms (guidance, counseling, student affairs, student development) that have been popular at various times.

Just as one of the historical roots of the community college was the push by university presidents to rid their institutions of responsibility for the first two years of college, the student affairs profession has strong historical roots in the push by faculty to rid themselves of certain student-oriented responsibilities. Thus, student records functions, advising, and discipline concerns, among others, were shifted gradually from faculty to specialized student affairs professionals. This movement can be traced from the late 1800s.

Rudolph (1962) indicated that the "whole apparatus of counseling" can be attributed to the creation of a system of faculty advising at Johns Hopkins in 1877 and to the appointment of freshmen advisors at Harvard in 1889. Over the course of the next 40 years, there was sufficient movement in the direction of creating separate offices or bureaus to handle student matters that, by 1937, the American Council on Education (ACE) issued a report entitled *The Student Personnel Point of View*. Chaired by E. G. Williamson, the ACE report outlined the philosophy, services, coordination, and future development of the emerging field of student affairs. The report became a guide for the profession and clearly stated an obligation of institutions of higher education to consider each student as a "whole person." The philosophy placed its emphasis on ". . . the development of the student as a person rather than upon his [sic] intellectual training alone." (*The Student Personnel Point of View*, cited in Saddlemire & Rentz, 1983, p. 76). The statement also listed 23 services that should be part of a student affairs program, including admissions, orientation, occupational advising, job placement, and housing.

In 1949, a second statement, also entitled *The Student Personnel Point of View*, was issued by ACE. Again chaired by Williamson, the committee that developed the report reaffirmed the basic philosophy of the 1937 report and expanded the statement of professional goals and objectives. These two reports were the major guides for the student affairs profession well into the 1960s (Saddlemire, 1983).

During the 1960s, the student affairs profession went through many changes. One of the major factors in those changes was student activities exhibited as campus protests. Institution leaders frequently responded to protests by expanding student affairs programs. Another major occurrence was the growing body of theory on human development, particularly the relationship of that theory to students in their college years.

This later development was one of the factors that caused a reexamination within the profession of the proper role for student affairs professionals, a reexamination that is continuing. With the publication in 1975 by the Council of Student Personnel Associations in Higher Education (COSPA) of "Student Development Services in Post-Secondary Education," the profession seemed to be taking a definite turn toward a student development orientation.[1] While appearing to be a new orientation, the idea of focusing on a student's personal development was consistent with the "whole person" emphasis put forth in both the 1937 and 1949 ACE statements. If there was a major difference, it was probably the availability of numerous theories of human development, research on those theories as they applied to the college-age students, and on the provision of models for the application of human development theories to the practice of student affairs.

Throughout its history, the field of student affairs has struggled to establish itself as a recognized profession. While

[1] In 1972, Brown published for the American College Personnel Association a very influential monograph entitled *Student Development in Tomorrow's Higher Education: A Return to the Academy*. This monograph laid the groundwork for much of the later movement toward student development.

the field as a whole has grown, as all of postsecondary education has grown, many of the original issues of the profession are still unresolved. The period between World War I and the Depression was perhaps the best opportunity for the student affairs profession to achieve its goals. [A supportive educational philosophy (i.e., the philosophy of John Dewey) was popular during that period, there was concern by leading figures in higher education for the reintegration of the academic (intellectual) and social (affective) development of students, and there was also significant organizational growth of the student affairs profession (Fenske, 1980a).] The Depression ended that era, and the profession, as a non-revenue producing entity, had to struggle to maintain itself. The historical movement favoring the bringing together of academic and social development of students faded. The student affairs profession, however, retained as one of its historical roots a close association with the goals of the liberal arts. This liberal arts root is frequently overlooked as an important part of the student affairs heritage.

While there have been, and are, many attempts at operationalizing an approach to education that truly deals with the whole person, a great deal of support for such integration is not currently apparent, even though professional staffs generally have adopted a student development approach. In 1973, the Carnegie Commission on Higher Education's report, *The Purposes and Performance of Higher Education in the United States*, concluded that "Totalism in the campus approach to students is, we believe, neither wise nor possible" (p. 17). Perhaps more disheartening than the Carnegie Commission's rejection of the holistic approach to the development of students has been the inability of the student affairs profession itself to provide a leadership role for successful implementation of a development-oriented approach to student services. Stamatakos and Rogers (1984), after reviewing the basic philosophical documents that have guided the profession (the 1937 and 1949 American Council of Education reports and the Council of Student Personnel Associations in Higher Education statement on *Student Development-Services in Post-Secondary Education*), concluded that the documents have resulted in ". . .discord and divisiveness within the profession, identity crisis for the individual practitioner, and confusion among faculty and administrators regarding student affairs necessity within and contribution to the collegiate experience" (p. 400). Fenske (1980b) emphasized the difficulties of the profession because of the orientation of academic leaders; that is, the majority of university leaders earned graduate degrees at institutions that placed little value on student affairs. Thus, there is a strong impetus for perpetuating a system favoring academic development at the (near) exclusion of any other developmental goals.

The student affairs profession has an admirable history of concern for students and their development. This focus on students has been a constant unifying force within the profession, and the prospects for having the goals of the profession be the mainstream of postsecondary education are not impossible even though major impediments exist. For example, the community college could be fertile ground for achieving a general focus on student development in all its educational programs. As has been indicated, the two-year college has a history of expanding educational opportunities, of faculty whose major function is teaching rather than research, and of commitment to innovation fostered in part by a lack of burdensome tradition.

Student Affairs in the Two-Year College

Unlike the American four-year college, which existed for over 150 years without a separate division of student services, the two-year college demonstrated an interest in student services nearly from the beginning of its existence. Early acknowledgement of the need for student services usually manifested itself as a commitment to guidance services. Although the commitment to student services in the two-year college has been routinely expounded, the degree of commitment has varied, and the evaluation of the effectiveness of student services within the two-year college has been inconsistent.

Matson (1983) found that guidance and counseling was included by nearly all major community college writers in a list of purposes of the two-year college. Koos (1925/1970), who published one of the earliest works on the two-year college, stressed the importance of the junior college as one means of providing students with the individual attention they needed. Two articles, which appeared in separate journals in California in 1929 and 1930 (Kemp, 1930; Wiersing & Koos, 1929-1930, both cited in Palinchak, 1973), indicated a need for counseling and guidance in two-year colleges beyond that thought necessary in four-year colleges.

During this early period, nearly all two-year colleges were private junior colleges. Their primary function was to provide the first two years of liberal arts education, and occupational programs were just emerging as a part of the curriculum. What seems clear from the literature of that time is the special need students in two-year colleges had for *guidance*. Thus, the emphasis appeared to have been a relatively narrow one of guiding students to the best possible academic decisions. According to Tillery and Deegan (1985), counseling and support services during this period (1900-1930) was a very minor function focused primarily on articulating transfer requirements. There does not appear to have been any indication that student affairs (or probably two-year colleges) assumed a role to promote student development directly.

Throughout the later growth period of two-year colleges, major writers continued to speak of the need for student services. Bogue (1950, cited in Matson, 1983), supported "orientation and guidance" as one of the six specific functions of the junior college. Even the Truman Commission on Higher Education's 1948 report held that counseling would play a major role in adapting instruction to the needs of the increasing number of students who would pursue postsecondary education (cited in Vaughan, 1983). Medsker (1960) concluded that the need for counseling assistance for two-year college students had been evident and addressed since the beginning of the junior college movement. Thornton (1966) and Blocker, Plummer, and Richardson (1965) agreed that guidance was more important in the two-year than in the four-year college because of the ". . . heterogeneity of the student body, the variety and complexity of decisions that students make, and the need for nonacademic services that support and give purpose to the efforts of students" (p. 239). A Carnegie Commission report (1970) on community colleges indicated that "Guidance is particularly crucial for students who attend community colleges" (p. 21). The need for strong student services in the two-year college continues to be advocated (Dassance, 1984-85; Elsner & Ames, 1983; Matson & Deegan, 1985; Nolan & Paradise, 1979; Vaughan, 1983). Yet the most support within the two-year college centered on the need to provide information (about academic and transfer requirements) and to guide students into appropriate career choices. The latter function became more critical as increasing numbers of students enrolled in two-year colleges. In a classic study of a two-year college, Clark (1960) noted the importance of the counseling and guidance function "because the routing and rerouting of students is an important part of the operation" (p. 98). Clark coined the term "cooling out" to describe the process whereby counselors helped students readjust to more realistic expectations than those they may have had originally.[2] Others (Blocker, Plummer, and Richardson, 1965; Bogue, 1950, cited in Matson, 1983; Koos, 1925/1970; Medsker, 1960) also supported this relatively narrow, albeit important, guidance function of student affairs in the two-year college.

In the middle 1960s, there were a number of studies of various aspects of student affairs functions in two-year colleges, the most comprehensive of which was conducted by Raines (1965, cited in Collins, 1967). Raines' major conclusion was that student affairs programs in two-year colleges were seriously inadequate. This study received much attention from community college educators and was the basis of a publication by the American Association of Community and Junior Colleges (AACJC) (Collins, 1967) that contained recommendations for program improvement in student services. Thurston, Zook, Neher, and Ingraham (1972), in another AACJC monograph, reported on the chief student affairs administrator in the community college. This publication, which reported on two studies (one in 1967 and one in 1969) of chief student affairs officers, also contained several recommendations for improving the student

---

[2] Clark (1980) has indicated that his original concept of cooling out was frequently confused with casting out. He defends the positive value of the cooling out function as one which provides alternatives and reduces aspirations in a "soft" way. Perhaps most importantly, Clark indicates that "any system of higher education that has to reconcile such conflicting values as equity, competence, and individual choice . . . has to effect compromise procedures that allows for some of each" (p. 30).

services programs. On the whole, the Thurston report was also quite critical of the state of student affairs services in community colleges.

Understaffing, lack of funds, lack of status within the institution—all these problems indicate that student personnel services are still generally perceived by top administration, faculty, and boards of trustees as peripheral rather than central to the educational task of the junior college. More serious yet is the implication that education is still defined by what takes place in the classroom, rather than in the lives of students. (p. 44)

Aside from being negative assessments of the state of student services in the two-year college, these studies report the role of student services as narrow. There was no apparent recognition of a role for student services (or for anyone within the community college?) to be concerned with the development of the *whole* student. These negative assessments of the services aspect of student affairs work in the two-year college came at just about the same time that the student affairs profession was poised to move toward a student development orientation. The historical juxtaposition of these events (a negative evaluation of basic services in two-year colleges and a move to a more comprehensive developmental orientation) may have conspired to cause, in part, the current confusion about the proper role of student services in the two-year college.

The early 1970s were an exciting time for student affairs professionals and for community college educators. The student affairs profession was embracing new theories of human development and humanistic psychology as the legitimizing forces needed to support a focus on concern for the whole student. Community college enrollment was increasing rapidly and community colleges were widely supported (including funding) and often hailed as the fair-haired child of postsecondary education. Tillery and Deegan (1985) indicated that the period from 1950 to 1970 in the history of community colleges was the time during which counseling and student support services had "near parity with instruction" (p. 71). While this is a debatable point, it does appear that the early 1970s were a positive period for student affairs services in community colleges.

In 1972, O'Banion and Thurston edited a book entitled *Student Development Programs in the Community Junior Colleges.* This book set a new direction for student service programs in community colleges that focused on the goals of student development. In describing the "emerging model" of student affairs work, O'Banion, Thurston, and Gulden (1972) placed the focus on helping students move toward self-fulfillment and responsible development and on the importance of the learning climate. The student affairs professional would be a "human development facilitator" who would direct attention to helping bring about positive changes in student behavior. The authors indicated that "the basic rationale that supports the importance of student personnel work in the junior college is that the 'student personnel point of view' and the 'junior college point of view' are one and the same" (p. 211). *The Student Personnel Point of View* referenced was the one first articulated by the American Council on Education report published in 1937. The "emerging model" theme also appeared as a major article in the November, 1972 issue of the *Junior College Journal* and received wide dissemination among community college educators.

In describing this new direction, O'Banion *et al.*, were consistent with the movement within the student affairs profession. Work within the American College Personnel Association focused on the need for the integration of academic and student affairs (i.e., concern for the whole person), clearly articulated in Brown's (1972) monograph, *Student Development in Tomorrow's Higher Education: A Return to the Academy.* The 1975 report on *Student Development Services in Post-secondary Education* was another example of the profession's direction. Perhaps most significant was the publication of a book by Miller and Prince (1976), *The Future of Student Affairs.* This book put forth a rationale for the practice of student affairs and a conceptual model for treating each student as a developing human being, recognizing and supporting all forms of development.

Within community colleges, it is difficult to gauge the degree to which the renewed focus on student development was implemented. Wolf and Dameron (1975), reporting on a comparative study of two-year and four-year counseling centers, found that the two-year counseling centers were more oriented to academic advisement than to other forms of counseling. Litwack (1978) and Miller (1979) found two-year counseling services generally to be pragmatic, focusing on coping skills and vocational and career counseling rather than on personal-social forms of counseling. These studies did not, however, address the broader question of the degree to which the student affairs program in two-year colleges might be focused on student development concerns.

Jonassen and Stripling's (1977) report on their study of student affairs practitioners in Florida community colleges provided some hint of a changing perspective within the two-year college. Using the 21 basic student services contained in the 1965 Raines study, Jonassen and Stripling used a Delphi technique to determine practitioners' opinions of current priorities for student services programs in two-year colleges. The authors concluded that there was a change in priorities from the 1965 list of services and that that change was toward student development and away from student regulation.

Steinke (1975) reported on a study of public community colleges to determine the degree to which they were involved in human development activities. He reported that 72% of the deans of students perceived themselves in the role of human development specialist. A large number of community colleges in the Steinke study also reported that the student affairs staff taught student development courses and that their counselors consulted with faculty regarding ways to facilitate students' development. Creamer (1985) reported on a survey of small, rural community colleges and concluded "that developmental purposes for student services are desired and, to a lesser extent, exist in actual practice, but that they are incorporated in a clearly subordinate manner to purposes of a basic service or career planning type" (p. 27).

There appears to be little doubt that student affairs professionals in community colleges have taken a more developmental perspective than in the past. Robbins (1983) described the hope and challenge for community college counselors and focused on the need to promote developmental change in students. A recent document adopted by the Deans of Students of Maryland Community Colleges (Slowinski, 1984) contained, as the first sentence on philosophy and purpose, the following: "The purpose of student services is to help create a learning environment that maximizes the development of the whole individual" (p. 6). Other philosophical statements describing student services programs contain similar language. It is also clear that community college leaders are unconvinced of the need to develop the whole student or the role student affairs plays in that process.

The Challenge for Leadership

Elsner and Ames (1983), among many today, are calling for a redesign of student services in two-year colleges. Matson and Deegan (1985), in considering student support services in two-year colleges, concluded that "a reassessment and agreement on mission and priorities . . ." (p. 147) is needed. Creamer (1985), while discussing the unclear purposes of student services, made a crucial point. Those outside the profession, he argued, "ponder whether such services and activities indeed are necessary educational pursuits . . ." (p. 30). Tillery and Deegan (1985) offered a rationale for a reversal of the growth of student services in the late 1960s. The expansion of services often occurred on the fringes of the mainstream of the institution, and new programs frequently were initiated by a splintering of personnel and functions. Thus, such programs have been particularly vulnerable to budget reductions and have helped create a paradox within the community college: At a time when there is general agreement on the need for an effective program of student services in the two-year college, many student affairs programs are being reduced in staff and other resources (Matson & Deegan, 1985).

The history of student services in the two-year college is tied closely to the history of the community college and to the history of the student affairs profession. The underlying philosophy of the student affairs profession is consistent with the philosophy and traditions of the comprehensive community college. Yet, the student affairs function within the two-year college has not overcome the same problems facing the profession as a whole: How to clearly articulate to key decision makers in the academic community the purpose and value of a concern for the development of the whole student and the role of student affairs within the mainstream of the institution to help achieve developmental outcomes for students.

Failure as yet to overcome such problems should not dissuade attempts within the profession to strive for success. The challenge exists for student services professionals in the two-year college to foster opportunities for students' development and to convince community college decision makers of the legitimacy—in fact the necessity—of focusing on broad, developmental goals for students. The remainder of this monograph will consider the nature of this challenge.

References

American Council on Education. (1983). The student personnel point of view. In G. L. Saddlemire & A. L. Rentz (Eds.), *Student affairs—A profession's heritage: Significant articles, authors, issues and documents* (pp. 74-87). Alexandria, VA: American College Personnel Association Media (Southern Illinois University Press). (Original work published 1937).

American Council on Education. (1983). The student personnel point of view. In G. L. Saddlemire & A. L. Rentz (Eds.), *Student affairs—A profession's heritage: Significant articles, authors, issues and documents* (pp. 122-140). Alexandria, VA: American College Personnel Association Media (Southern Illinois University Press). (Original work published 1949).

Blocker, C. E., Plummer, R. H., & Richardson, R. C., Jr. (1965). *The two-year college: A special synthesis.* Englewood Cliffs, NJ: Prentice-Hall.

Brown, R. D. (1972). *Student development in tomorrow's higher education: A return to the academy.* Washington, DC: American College Personnel Association (Monograph).

Carnegie Commission on Higher Education. (1970). *The open door colleges.* New York: McGraw-Hill.

Carnegie Commission On Higher Education. (1979). *The purposes and performance of higher education in the United States.* New York: McGraw-Hill.

Clark, B. R. (1960). *The open door college: A case study*. New York: McGraw-Hill.

Clark, B. R. (1980). The "cooling out" function revisited. In G. B. Vaughan (Ed.), *Questioning the community college role*. (New Directions Monograph #32). San Francisco: Jossey-Bass.

Cohen, A. M., & Brawer, F. B. (1982). *The American community college*. San Francisco: Jossey-Bass.

Collins, C. C. (1967). *Junior college student personnel programs: What they are and what they should be*. Washington, DC: American Association of Community and Junior Colleges.

Council of Student Personnel Associations in Higher Education. (1975). Student development services in post-secondary education. *Journal of College Student Personnel, 16*(6), 524-528.

Creamer, D. C. (1985). How developmental are community college student personnel purposes? *Community College Review, 12*(4), 27-30.

Dassance, C. R. (1984-85). Community college student personnel work: Is the model still emerging? *Community College Review, 12*(3), 25-29.

Elsner, P. A., & Ames, W. C. (1983). Redirecting student services. In G. B. Vaughn (Ed.), *Issues for community college leaders in a new era*. San Francisco: Jossey-Bass.

Fenske, R. H. (1980a). Historical foundations. In U. Delworth, G. R. Hanson & Associates (Eds.), *Student services: A handbook for the profession*. San Francisco: Jossey-Bass.

Fenske, R. H. (1980b). Current trends. In U. Delworth, G. R. Hanson & Associates (Eds.), *Student services: A handbook for the profession*. San Francisco: Jossey-Bass.

Jonassen, E. O., & Stripling, R. O. (1977). Priorities for community college student personnel services during the next decade. *Journal of College Student Personnel, 18*(2), 83-86.

Koos, L. V. (1970). *The junior college movement*. New York: AMS Press. (Original work published in 1925.)

Litwack, L. (1978). Counseling services in community colleges. *Journal of College Student Personnel, 19*(4), 359-361.

Matson, J. E. (1983). Primary roles for community college counselors. In A. S. Thurston & W. A. Robbins (Eds.), *Counseling: A crucial function for the 1980's*. (pp. 19-28). San Francisco: Jossey-Bass.

Matson, J. E., & Deegan, W. L. (1985). Revitalizing student services. In W. L. Deegan & D. Tillery (Eds.), *Renewing the American community college.* San Francisco: Jossey-Bass.

Medsker, L. L. (1960). *The junior college: Progress and prospect.* New York: McGraw-Hill.

Medsker, L. L., & Tillery, D. (1971). *Breaking the access barriers: A profile of two-year colleges.* New York: McGraw-Hill.

Miller, T. K., & Prince, J. S. (1976). *The future of student affairs.* San Francisco: Jossey-Bass.

Miller, T. M. (1979). A study of counseling services in two-year colleges. *Journal of College Student Personnel. 20*(1), 9-14.

Monroe, C. R. (1972). *Profile of the community college.* San Francisco: Jossey-Bass.

Naisbitt, J., & Aburdene, P. (1985). *Re-inventing the corporation.* New York: Warner Books.

Nolan, E. J., & Paradise, L. V. (1979). An overview of community college counseling. *Journal of College Student Personnel. 20*(5), 398-402.

O'Banion, T., Thurston, A., & Gulden, J. (1970). Student personnel work: An emerging model. *Junior College Journal. 41*(3), 6-13.

O'Banion, T., & Thurston, A. (1972). *Student development programs in the community junior college.* Englewood Cliffs, NJ: Prentice-Hall.

Palinchak, R. (1973). *The evolution of the community college.* Metuchen, NJ: The Scarecrow Press.

Robbins, W. A. (1983). Counseling for today's community college students. In A. S. Thurston & W. A. Robbins, (Eds.), *Counseling: A crucial function for the 1980's.* (New Directions Monograph #43). San Francisco: Jossey-Bass.

Rudolph, R. (1962). *The American college and university: A history.* New York: Vintage Books.

Saddlemire, G. L. (1983). Professional developments. In U. Delworth, G. R. Hanson & Associates (Eds.), *Student services: A handbook for the profession* (pp. 25-44). San Francisco: Jossey-Bass.

Saddlemire, G. L., & Rentz, A. L. (Eds.). (1983). *Student affairs— A profession's heritage: Significant articles, authors, issues and documents.* Alexandria, VA: American College Resource Association Media.

Slowinski, D. J. (Ed.) (1984). *A guide for effective student services in Maryland community colleges.* (A monograph adopted by the Deans of Students of the Maryland Community Colleges.) Baltimore: Essex Community College.

Staff. (1984, March 6). Indicators brief. Supplement to the *AAC-JC Letter, 82.* Washington, DC: American Association of Community and Junior Colleges.

Staff. (1985, April 15). Twenty years of growth. Supplement to the *AACJC Letter, 45.* Washington, DC: American Association of Community and Junior Colleges.

Stamatakos, L. C., & Rogers, R. R. (1984). Student affairs: A profession in need of a philosophy. *Journal of College Student Personnel, 25*(5), 400-411.

Steinke, R. J. (1975). *Human development education in community junior colleges.* Littleton, CO: Developmental Dynamics.

Thornton, J. W., Jr. (1966). *The community junior college* (2nd ed.). New York: John Wiley & Sons.

Thurston, A. J., Zook, F. B., Neher, T., & Ingraham, J. (1972). *The chief student personnel administrator in the public two-year college.* (ERIC Clearinghouse for Junior Colleges: Monograph Series #14). Washington, DC: American Association of Community and Junior Colleges.

Tillery, D., & Deegan, W. L. (1985). The evolution of two-year colleges through four generations. In W. L. Deegan & D. Tillery (Eds.), *Renewing the American community college* (pp. 3-33). San Francisco: Jossey-Bass.

Vaughan, G. B. (1982). *The community college in America: A pocket history.* Washington, DC: American Association of Community and Junior Colleges.

Vaughan, G. B. (1983). President Truman endorsed community college manifesto. *Community and Junior College Journal 53*(7), 21-24.

Wolf, J. C., & Dameron, J. D. (1975). Counseling center functions in two-year and four-year colleges. *Journal of College Student Personnel, 16*(6), 482-485.

Chapter 2

Opportunities in Diversity

Steven R. Helfgot

Diversity may well be the most descriptive label that can be attached to America's community colleges. They differ from other types of colleges in such characteristics as curriculum focus and length, and they vary within the type by the range of student characteristics and demands for specialized service from their communities.

Even in a pluralistic system of higher education, community colleges are distinguishable by these characteristics. America itself is composed of multiple ethnic, racial, religious, and social subcultures, and each is encouraged to participate autonomously in society. Higher education in America is structured to recognize, to use, and to benefit by this reality. Yet, it may be said of the community college that it is perhaps the most varied of all institutional types.

The community college is located everywhere—often within an hour's drive of every citizen in some states. It is in the city and on the farm. It is where the people are. Since many of the nation's community colleges were created as community projects ("We want our own college" often served as a battle cry in state houses where requests were made for legislative support), it is not surprising that they are flavored by community characteristics unlike some other types of colleges which were flavored by more universal, traditional, and conventional perspectives of higher learning.

Arising from such an array of local perspectives, the community college can boast of its responsiveness to local needs and of how its curriculum often is shaped by those needs. Yet its curriculum must be responsive to other needs as well, such as the obligation to prepare students to transfer to other colleges and universities.

In operational terms, the community college is subject to many of the same social, economic, and political pressures as all other types of colleges; however, community colleges remain different because of two realities: (a) the requests for service, such as specific manpower training, are substantially different from those of other types of colleges or universities; and (b) the characteristics of the students who attend are different from students who attend other colleges or universities in *range of characteristics*, in the comparatively short-term *nature of certain career aspirations*, and in *attendance patterns*.

The focus of this chapter will be on the differences in students that justify the claim of diversity in community colleges.

Gleazer (1980) described community college students as ". . . the same people we meet in the shops and offices and plants. They govern the city and install the telephones. They deliver the papers and repair the cars" (pp. 10-11). Community college students always have been a cross section of adults in America and have been consistently described in this manner by prominent community college educators (Cohen & Brawer, 1982; Collins, 1972; Cross, 1972; Monroe, 1972; Thornton, 1966; Thurston, 1972; Vaughan, 1985).

Community college student characteristics are notable by their range. Students from the lowest and the highest social strata of society and those gifted with intellectual superiority seek community college instruction regularly, and those of every ethnic and social subculture are present for formal and informal educational experiences. Community college students often enroll for career-oriented purposes of short duration. They may experiment with further education, or they may pursue occupational education or training of a one- or two-year period. Finally, they attend the community college in patterns that vary significantly from convention. Unlike the conventional pattern of attending full-time during the day, community college students often attend part-time and whenever their other life activities permit a few hours to direct to education. Their attendance is sporadic and is almost always woven into a life fabric consisting of many other interests and obligations. They are likely to give only a piece of themselves to education and reserve the rest for the pursuit of other interests and aspirations.

While obviously overstating, Collins (1972) captured another perspective on community college students when he characterized them as neither committed to intellectual values nor looking for an intellectual atmosphere. Yet it would be illogical to assume that students of such diversity would not, in part, lack many values of conventional higher education. The fact is that most students, including community college students, embrace competing values for education: learning for knowledge and learning for utility, education as primary and education as secondary among life's priorities, and education as the preserver of culture and education as innovator.

So what? What does student diversity on the community college campus mean? Of what importance or value is it to the student affairs profession? Answers to those questions are perspective-bound. Diversity can be seen by professionals as an insurmountable *problem* or as an *opportunity* holding potential to aid students. While a premise of this chapter is that opportunity resides in diversity, the realities of problems inherent in the condition will not be underestimated.

Working with Diversity

The student affairs profession was born on the college campus. As it grew and evolved, it did so in the context of the typical 18- to 22-year-old residential student who was its primary constituent. It was not an easy nor a problem-free task to adjust professional services designed for traditional students and traditional enrollment patterns to diverse students, attending nontraditionally, and who commute to campus. The problem can be seen by examining several traditional student affairs functions.

Counseling and student activities are among the most traditional of student service functions. They can be used to illustrate the problems of student diversity in the community college.

Most community college counselors—perhaps with the exception of those trained since the mid-1970s—were trained to deal with young people or traditional students. As adults of all ages with a seemingly infinite variety of life experiences invaded the community college, many counselors have felt ill-prepared and uncomfortable, finding that adult students have different counseling and advising needs than younger students.

Diversity among students is the source of still other problems in the counseling area. Staff work schedules, for example, must be adapted to the nonconventional attendance patterns of students. Community college students generally are not in residence, do not attend full-time, nor attend during the day. College is but one priority in their lives. They have jobs and families. They come to campus to take classes and, though they may need counseling, advising, or testing, they may not request it for lack of time. Their available time may be in the evening or on a weekend. Counselors who work from 9 to 5, Monday through Friday, will not reach these students.

Counseling appears to have been the kind of service attractive to middle and upper-middle class students. The helping professions generally have appealed more to those of higher socioeconomic status. In the traditional collegiate environment, counseling is more marketable than in the community college where some portion of the student body may have no experience with counseling services and may be suspicious, if not hostile, to the very idea of being counseled.

The problems are no less real in the area of student activities. This extracurricular area traditionally has been viewed as the provider of recreation and entertainment on the college campus for the student body. Student activities are most effective with captive audiences on residential campuses. The community college audience is not captive. In fact, these students may spend the minimum amount of time possible on the campus. They are not homogeneous socially, recreationally, or culturally. And the college usually exists in the same community where the students live, making the recreational resources of the community a readily available alternative.

Diversity of students certainly causes problems for student affairs professionals. Just because problems exist, however, does not mean that they should be used as a reason to desist from the task. In fact, as much as the significant diversity among community college students is a problem, it is even more a resource and an opportunity to enhance students' development.

How so? In diversity there is richness, a breadth and depth of human experience, that can be used, as students interact with one another both formally and informally, to expand and intensify existing opportunities and create new ones for learning. Interactions such as these enrich learning. Gleazer (1980) has described those conditions as advantageous to student learning, referring specifically to numerous program options, and to an environment in which there is a mix of generations, ethnic backgrounds, and socioeconomic characteristics. The student affairs profession plays a key role here—tapping the resources in the diversity of students, and finding ways to make the best use of the opportunities that diversity provides. This is a multifaceted task that should be undertaken through creative administrative organization, meaningful relationships between the student affairs and the rest of the institution, and novel approaches to performing student affairs functions.

Administrative organization is at once irrelevant and crucial. It is irrelevant because a student affairs staff, sensitive to diversity and responsive to students' needs, will find ways to be successful and to work toward student development goals regardless of organizational structure. On the other hand, organization may be crucial because structure often is a signal about what is important, valuable, and seen as a priority. Hence, a traditional structure may send a message to nontraditional students as to their relative importance to student affairs. Groups of students who believe that their needs are seen as unimportant may well disassociate themselves from student affairs programs, or never bother with it in the first place. This can be a significant burden with which to contend and difficult to overcome.

Organization can enhance opportunities to promote development in students if it is characterized by several important factors.

1. The professional staff should be composed of more generalists than specialists, people with a variety of skills and background experience. They should be able to function well in more than one student affairs area and should be competent in multiple intervention strategies and knowledgeable about developmental and social theory.

2. The organization should encourage regular and significant interactions among its various units, offices, and staff. Sharing information about students seems particularly critical when student subpopulations may vary as much as they do in community colleges.

3. A viable student affairs organization must be outreach oriented. Diverse student populations will congregate in different locations on the campus; some subpopulations will not congregate on the campus at all but may be found in various places throughout the community. The organizational units must inhabit a number of different places on the campus and extend themselves to the cafeteria, the library, the academic support center, the gym, the student center, and the adult resource office. They should also inhabit locations in the community, such as churches, recreation centers, libraries, shopping centers, and even street corners.

4. The organization should employ students. Younger students from divergent groups, adults—both men and women, minorities, students of all sorts might work as peer counselors, tutors, student activities assistants, and in other capacities. These student employees can provide two distinct advantages to the student affairs unit. First, they can provide a contact point for many students, an entrance for those students into the college's support service system. Second, student support services can be modified and adjusted to meet the needs of the various subgroups through the feedback received from students of various subgroups who get into the system and from the student employees themselves.

All these organizational characteristics do not themselves create special opportunities for student development, but they can help mold an environment or learning climate in which the opportunities provided by diversity can be exploited. If the organization invites students of all sorts to make contact, opportunity is enhanced.

The purpose of these organizational accommodations is to encourage students' development in a comprehensive sense of that term: to create opportunities for students of diverse backgrounds to enhance their intellectual, social, psychological, interpersonal, moral, cultural, and aesthetic development. Some of these opportunities can be provided through standard areas within student affairs. However, in order truly to maximize opportunities and to use the resource of diversity to its fullest, relationships must be built between student affairs and other areas of the college, especially the academic area.

Organizational Integration

Even if they find one another nowhere else on campus, students of every type will, of necessity, encounter one another in the classroom. In many classes, students remain isolated from each other—responding only to the instructor, doing assignments, or taking tests—and the potential for powerful interaction among students is lost. Student affairs professionals can promote student interactions if allowed to work with faculty in classes. For example, they might be invited to help with projects, with experientially-based learning tasks, as with simulation exercises.

Further, student affairs staff may be helpful in translating student experience in a learning situation by being sensitive to student developmental stages, or to pressures that may affect classroom performance, attendance patterns, or the lead time required to get an assignment done.

A similar opportunity exists in the building of course schedules, the sequencing of classes, and in organizing a particular curriculum. An important question arises in these activities: Are the needs, skills, experiences, and concerns of various groups of students being accounted for? If there are large numbers of working students in a particular academic program, are sufficient courses from that program offered in the evening? Are courses that have prerequisites scheduled so that students will not have to wait a year before the course they need is again offered? Are courses in a given curriculum sequenced in such a manner that the load will be balanced from term to term? This is of great concern to students who also need to balance school, work, family, and other priorities. Student affairs professionals should know these students and their concerns; they can be of help—albeit indirectly—by conveying what they know about students to curriculum planners and schedule builders in the institution.

While all this is important to the goal of student development, the various student affairs functional areas provide the most potential for capitalizing upon diversity, though there seems to be some controversy about how best to do this. One approach is a back to basics or no frills philosophy of student affairs in the community college. The argument is this: There is a wide range of students with an even wider range of needs. Those needs are primarily related to academic and career goals. Therefore, student affairs should concentrate all of its efforts on those functions that serve those needs and on assessment, feedback, counseling, advising, and teaching. Master these activities, provide them in ways that are appropriate to a particular student population, and do not waste time on anything else. According to this argument, this will help both individual students and students in the aggregate and focuses attention and resources on that which is most important to their primary goals.

This argument is solid and represents a valid approach, especially in an era of diminishing resources and shrinking enrollments. However, there is an equally valid and perhaps more persuasive argument: The way to maximize the opportunities for student development found in diversity is by providing the greatest possible number of contact points for students—contact points where they can encounter both one another and an array of services. That can best be done through a wide range of student services. There will be multiple foci: student activities, advising and counseling, academic support services, career placement, and instruction, among others.

Student activities represents a powerful organizational tool to deal with diversity and is too often overlooked. A community college student activities program can be the major vehicle for developing a sense of community on campus. A student government that must address the needs of all students can bring those various students together, talking, benefitting from one another's experiences, enriching the whole program. This idea was captured by James:

> The most visible procedure for developing one student body on campuses is through extracurricular activities. Diversity of interests within the student body on a community college campus makes such activities important. Student organizations that cross curricular lines should be emphasized. Student government, campus newspapers, intramural sports, hobby and interest clubs, vocal and instrumental music, radio, photography, plays and concerts, dances, parties, and mixers form natural situations for developing understanding, communications, and oneness within a community college student body. (James, 1982, p. 20)

This notion, of course, is not new. Collins saw the potential a decade ago when he wrote

> Junior colleges . . . should develop . . . such an attractive co-curricular program that it will seduce even the practical minded, working, commuting student. As a matter of fact, it is just such a student who should be exposed to . . . new ideas and life styles and lured into new cultural and intellectual experiences. (Collins, in O'Banion, 1972, p. 15)

Community college students are consumers. If they are paying an activities fee, they expect something for it. Yet rock and roll bands do not meet the recreational needs of adults. Daytime programming or even on-campus evening programs do not provide for the in-and-out evening student. Very little of a recreational nature attracts the student taking only one course. Yet these students are elected to student governments, or they come to student activities offices and ask for something of value in return for fees paid. A broad view of student activities is required to offer the best response to such requests.

Responding to special requests for service from students of

diverse backgrounds and needs may result in far-ranging programming. Thus, diversity of student characteristics, requiring tailored responses from professionals, may serve to enrich the nature of educational service. This relationship of student need to professional response may be illustrated by the case of women returning to school who organize student clubs, seek funding, and bring speakers to campus to address problems of balancing career and family. Other students, either on their own or through a class, attend that presentation—an opportunity created by diversity. When a college-wide wellness program is put in place and students of all ages participate in physical fitness activities, and students from different socioeconomic and ethnic groups are exposed to ideas of good health and prevention with which they were previously unfamiliar, an opportunity has been created because of diversity. When a college uses its community to meet the needs of diverse populations by purchasing and making available to students tickets for the theater, the symphony, the ballet, art, and museum exhibits, an opportunity has been created because of diversity. When the leaders of various student clubs and organizations come together for leadership training or to conduct business—each representing a unique constituency—then another opportunity has been created. And each of these examples is but an illustration of the greater potential.

Very often, student development opportunities emanate from the counseling staff and their work. Counselors work extensively in an academic advising capacity, for example. Academic advising in its fullest sense is developmental life planning that involves the student in examining life goals, lifestyle choices, and career aspirations, as well as program and course choices. Students are sometimes limited in their ability to participate in this process by the limitations of their own backgrounds and life experiences. When counselors organize advising groups with a mix of students, the life planning process is enriched by interactions with others who have different perspectives on life. Such interactions often result in the enhancement of development and academic achievement through enlightened intellectual or cognitive awareness.

Counselors also work with students in vocational instructional programs. Those programs often draw students different from those in academic areas. Some students have work experience in the vocational field but are not experienced in or have had poor experiences with education. For others, the opposite is true. If counselors, in advising students, could get these students talking with each other, students may be able to overcome disadvantages associated with their experiences and maximize their special qualities.

Much the same is true of other kinds of counseling provided on the community college campus. Any group or workshop, such as assertiveness training or stress management, may be more productive if students with different experiences participate. There are special counseling opportunities created by diversity. Groups in which younger and older students deal with family or relationship questions provide much greater opportunity for growth and understanding than do those in which the population is more homogeneous. The other side can be presented by those who are actually experiencing it.

Finally, peer counselors drawn from various peer groups on campus can be an exceptional asset. The benefit of student employees has been discussed previously. Nowhere is their potential impact so great as in the case of peer counselors. They can be used in outreach, in intake processing, in advising other student groups, and in translating needs of a particular group of students to professional providers of service. Peer counselors serve as models to other students to promote understanding of self and of the institution.

Academic support services, such as tutoring, provide much the same kind of opportunity as counseling and advising. Students may require academic assistance of several types. Some will need help in understanding textbook material, for example, or how to write a term paper. Others may need assistance in practical applications (particularly in vocational program areas) or in laboratory work. Students with different backgrounds and of different ages, with varied skills and experiences, may need assistance in one area while being able to give assistance in another. If situations can be created wherein students can trade assistance with each other, then there is a benefit, not just in student learning, but in the mutual respect and understanding that different students can have for one another.

Career placement is another area rich in opportunity for working with diverse student populations. Community colleges are populated with students who are working or who have worked in businesses, industries, and services. Some have been employers; even more have been through the interview and hiring process as employees. At the other end of the spectrum are the many community college students with no work experience or with only part-time work experience. Many of these students are ignorant about the world of work, have no understanding of the ethics of the workplace, and know nothing about interview behavior. The well-informed and experienced student could provide a much needed service for those lacking in experience. Neither resume writing workshops, written guides to interview behavior, films, nor video tapes are as valuable as the experience of those who have worked in a particular industry to helping those who wish to enter it. Interview simulations, guides to negotiating a salary, an insider's view of a particular corporation, and general information on survival and advancement in the workplace could all be provided through the career placement office using students in the institution with appropriate credentials.

The student affairs staff may have instructional responsibilities, such as workshops and seminars, orientation courses, or human development courses. As indicated earlier, if students of different backgrounds encounter one another nowhere else on campus, they will surely do so in the classroom. The opportunities for meaningful interaction here are abundant.

In an orientation class, for example, students may struggle, in the transition to college, with their fears and inadequacies. Often students will think that such problems and fears are uniquely their own or unique to their type of student. This, on occasion, leads to isolation. Alliances and support systems can be built and new understandings arrived at when younger and older students—those who have been out of school and those who have been in, those planning to transfer and those in terminal programs—all discover that they share similar fears, doubts, and concerns.

In personal development courses, the potential for growth

is also enhanced when differing perspectives are brought to bear on a problem or subject. The late adolescent who has trouble communicating with parents may find that a classmate who is a peer of his/her parents is easy to talk to, understanding, and open. Conversely, the adult student having trouble understanding children in late adolescence may gain valuable insight, information, and perspective from a fellow student in the same life stage as his/her children.

The Challenge of Leadership

Since diversity among community college students provides unique opportunities for promoting student development, how can leaders in student affairs take advantage of these opportunities?

First, chief student affairs officers must think about diversity among their students as a source of opportunity. Too often the presence of numerous subpopulations on campus, each with a variety of needs that seem to be at odds with one another, may paralyze a student affairs unit or overwhelm it, resulting in organizational inertia or in services reduced to the lowest common denominator. If these numerous subpopulations are considered positively, numerous possibilities for creative and effective programs and services may appear.

In an era when enrollments are dropping and student services require justification for use of scarce resources, it is imperative for student affairs leaders to take advantage of every opportunity that demonstrates the value and effect of their work. Thinking about possibilities rather than problems is a first step in that direction.

A related challenge is conducting those assessments necessary to make sense of the diversity that exists. Clearly defining the significant subgroups on campus and the range of pertinent characteristics of subpopulations is a necessary step to developing programs and services that meet the needs of the various subgroups of students. The same care needs to be taken with the individual assessment of students. Not only students' academic aptitude, but their intellectual reasoning ability, learning style, preference, career development, and moral development, among others, should be assessed to develop programs and help students establish goals. The student affairs professional should also communicate this information to others in the institution who could use it to benefit students. Faculty, for example, should be interested in the learning style preferences of students and in the status of students' intellectual development. The challenge for student affairs professionals is to be able to describe accurately the range of diversity among students in a way that is meaningful to others and to guide program development.

Student affairs leaders must recognize student diversity when hiring and assigning staff. Student affairs staff cannot be hired nor can staffing patterns be developed with only the traditional student in mind. Staff with diverse backgrounds and broad-based training are needed, especially training in counseling and career development, student development, adult development theory, outreach techniques, and the dynamics of family systems. Staff must know and understand not only higher education and the community college but also have a variety of life and work experiences outside education. Above all, staff are needed who are able and willing to work creatively with different student populations in different settings using a variety of intervention techniques, including instruction, counseling, programming, and consultation. Maximizing opportunities in diversity requires student affairs professionals to define their roles broadly and approach their duties creatively.

When opportunities exist to hire staff members, the task is perhaps somewhat easier. However, in many community college student affairs divisions, veteran staff members' professional education and training may fall short of what has been suggested. Thus, the third challenge to student affairs leaders is to provide a staff development program to train and retrain student affairs staff so that they will be able to meet the needs of diverse students. It is not enough to have skilled professionals with good hearts and a willingness to meet student needs (though that is certainly requisite). There are theories to be applied, ideas that must be taught, and new skills that must be acquired. If those in leadership roles are serious about serving all students, then staff training opportunities must be created.

A fourth challenge for student affairs leaders in this area is to take charge in planning, establishing priorities, making assignments, and in supporting professional development activities. Leadership is required. Rewards must be given consistent with organizational goals. The leadership message must not be one of maintenance only or providing basic service conservatively. Diversity among students must be viewed as a resource, and clear messages must be given to expand, to innovate, and to use the diversity in the student body.

Student affairs professionals have a significant opportunity to provide leadership for the college in having the diversity of students considered as an institutional asset. Community colleges have a heritage of providing opportunities to a wide range of students. It is a continuing challenge to build on that heritage in a way that provides opportunities to an even broader range of students. Student affairs professionals can take the lead in meeting that challenge.

References

Cohen, A. M. & Brawer, F. B. (1982). *The American community college*. San Francisco: Jossey-Bass.

Collins, C. C. (1972). Student characteristics and their implications for student personnel work. In T. O'Banion and A. Thurston (Eds.), *Student development programs in the community junior college*. Englewood Cliffs, NJ: Prentice-Hall.

Cross, K. P. (1972). Higher education's newest student. In T. O'Banion and A. Thurston (Eds.), *Student development programs in the community junior college*. Englewood Cliffs, NJ: Prentice Hall.

Gleazer, E. J. (1980). *The community college: Values, visions and vitality*. Washington: American Association of Community and Junior Colleges.

James, G. B. (1982). Democracy in action—How to create one student body in a community college. *Community College Review, 9*(4), 19-21.

Monroe, C. R. (1972). *Profile of the community college*. San Francisco: Jossey-Bass.

Thornton, J. W., Jr. (1966). *The community junior college* (2nd Edition). New York: John Wiley and Sons.

Thurston, A. (1972). The decade ahead. In T. O'Banion and A. Thurston (Eds.). *Student development programs in the community junior college.* Englewood Cliffs, NJ: Prentice-Hall.

Vaughan, G. B. & Associates. (1983). *Issues for community college leaders in a new era.* San Francisco: Jossey-Bass.

Chapter 3

Opportunities Through Interdependence

Edward W. Phoenix, R. Thomas Flynn, Deborah L. Floyd

In the four decades since World War II, community colleges have grown from a handful of institutions to more than 1,200 colleges serving 5,000,000 students annually. This phenomenal growth was not without some negative consequences. Cosand (1979), for example, suggested that the rapid growth of enrollments, in concert with the diversity of the student populations and a lack of clarity and commitment to institutional missions, led critics to characterize community colleges as the "educational slums" of postsecondary education. The community college response, Cosand suggested, was influenced by the fact that "community college faculty and administrators have, for the most part, wanted to be considered as a part of the higher education community and to be respected as peers by their four-year college and university counterparts" (p. 3).

To counteract the critics' perceptions, therefore, many in the community college field placed emphasis on certain aspects of professionalism and autonomy to enhance their status in higher education. Thus, individual faculty tended to identify themselves more with their particular disciplines than with their institutions and, similarly, staff tended to affiliate more with specialists in their fields of expertise than with other administrative colleagues in their own colleges. Concurrently, many community colleges (most notably those receiving public support) tended to de-emphasize their affiliations with nonacademic agencies and institutions in an effort to gain greater acceptance and respect within academe.

We believe that individuals and postsecondary institutions have focused too narrowly on specialization and independence to develop images of quality and prestige. Professional development and autonomy are associated with other elements that must be considered as community college educators strive to improve their roles, contributions, and recognition within the higher education community.

Quality and Prestige Through Interdependence

While acknowledging specialized research and scholarship as the central trunk that must be preserved on the "professional development tree," Lindquist (1981) suggested a number of interactive "branches" that also must be included in the development of the professional person. His model for holistic professional development emphasizes "social learning," including knowledge of institutional mission; political, economic, and cultural trends; community and organizational factors affecting the institution; student biographical characteristics and learning needs; and alternative educational practices and research findings in postsecondary education. In all of these elements, a need to overcome the restrictiveness of specialization through intensive interaction with individual and institutional interdependencies is recognized.

According to Cross (1981), the development of autonomy, or the ability to be self-reliant and free from dependence, is an essential goal of learning. It must not, however, be taken to the point of denying integrative thinking. To do so would run the risk of parochialism, narrowness of vision, and isolation. Similarly, from an institutional standpoint, Cosand (1979) observed that "for a college to force the issue of autonomy against the best interests of the group and against the well-documented facts of governmental agencies would appear to be ill-advised and insensitive to reality" (p. 46). Rather, there must be a holistic perception that recognizes linkages and the need to cooperate for common purposes with others in larger systems. A recognition of the need for interdependence does not result in a denial of autonomy. In fact, from an institutional perspective, autonomy can be strengthened through interdependent relationships.

The foregoing suggests that individuals and community colleges may have focused on inappropriate elements of professional development and autonomy in their quest for quality and prestige. A question remains as to whether a holistic approach and acceptance of interdependence can enable individuals and institutions to attain these goals.

Vaughan (1983) declared that "if institutional integrity is to be maintained, quality . . . must be defined in terms that are compatible with the college's mission" (p. 13). Kuh (1981) observed that not only is quality a function of a clear, coherent, and consistent purpose, but that "nothing short of a holistic approach characterized by multiple data sources . . . can be afforded, if accurate and useful estimates of quality are expected" (p. 31). A review of the increasing number of reports on the quality and success of programs developed by means of interdivisional cooperation within colleges and extramural collaboration with community agencies, businesses and industry, and governmental units also strongly supports this contention. Thus, it seems that an understanding of mission, a recognition of the value of interdependence, and cooperative effort will lead to the development of what Kuh (1981) described as a "generative learning community"—an environment that enhances the quality, success, prestige, and service provided by community colleges.

All of the foregoing has been presented as justification for the basic premise of this chapter: interdependent relationships should be valued by community colleges for the opportunities they provide to enhance the quality and prestige of the institution. Most importantly, interdependent relationships should be valued for the opportunities they provide for enhancing development in students.

Perspectives on Community College Interdependence

Community colleges may be considered potentially the most interdependent type of institution in the field of higher education. Their basic mission and sources of funding demand involvement with their local communities, business and industry, and community and governmental agencies. With missions of providing senior college transfer education, vocational/technical education and training, and community services/continuing education programs, community college successes are dependent on effective relationships with agencies, secondary schools, senior colleges and universities, local employers, and the community at large.

The pervasiveness and complexity of interdependent relationships prohibit a comprehensive listing and inhibit their categorization. In considering perspectives on community college interdependence, the authors will review interdependence as it relates to students, faculty and staff, and to the community.

The Student Perspective. The primary interdependent relationship in any educational institution is between the institution and its students. In a broad sense, students include anyone who participates in any learning activity, on or off campus. As Floyd and Weihe (1985) assert, community colleges have been too limited in their description of and commitment to their total student populations. Typically, full consideration is given only to the student who is enrolled in credit courses, either for preparation for work or to transfer to a senior college. Student affairs professionals seem to devote little attention to students enrolled in noncredit, continuing education programs, that is, the adult basic education student, the student enrolled in a short-term word processing class, and the student learning via television in a home setting. Accepting a broad definition of student, community colleges may have been guilty of presenting a fragmented view of services. Community colleges rarely provide assessment, counseling, advisement, and follow-up services to students in nontraditional settings, such as in off-campus centers, homes, and business/industry sites or through television instruction.

Unfortunately, out-of-sight—out-of-mind seems to shape prevailing commitments. Students enrolled on campus seem to receive more support and more service than those enrolled in off-campus and nontraditional settings, indicating an acceptance of the interdependent relationship with traditional credit students while ignoring other students.

The interests and needs of all students must be evaluated regularly, and appropriate assessment/placement procedures, remedial/developmental programs, academic curricula, and student development services must be provided for a wide range of intellectual, psychological, cognitive, ability, age, and interest levels. Supportive counseling, interactive advisement by faculty and staff, and systematic intervention procedures are essential to the students' educational and vocational success. Just as courses and programs should be offered at times and in places convenient for students and faculty, services also should be extended, well publicized, and readily accessible to all.

Inherent in these concerns is the need for colleges to meet student expectations for occupational preparation and/or transfer education. Vocational skills training must be appropriate and up-to-date for the extant job market. Additionally, there must be some guarantee, either through articulation agreements or documentable records of success, of the transferability of credit to specific senior colleges.

More than a decade ago, O'Banion (1971) suggested that these college concerns must also be the concerns of student affairs. In his model, "student development specialists" served as change agents and catalysts who conducted research on student behavior, understood the complexity of the institution and the diverse student subcultures, and had a strong sense of mission and commitment to facilitate the development of all groups in the educational community. These are the same individuals who Cosand (1979) later described as "enlightened and highly qualified student services personnel [who] are essential to help define and explain the needs of students to the faculty, administration, and board" (p. 14).

In recent years, a number of unique programs have been developed that indicate a growing recognition of these concerns. For example, Central Piedmont Community College in Charlotte, North Carolina established a network of Area Learning Centers that offer traditional campus-based services to off-campus learners. Similarly, perhaps as an outgrowth of earlier marketing/recruitment efforts, a number of community colleges have recognized the benefits of community-based services through the establishment of information booths and registration facilities in local shopping malls. Triton College in suburban Chicago has proven the success of such activities when staffed by student personnel professionals and admissions personnel (Knight & Orozco, 1983).

A program option, entitled "Tuesday-Thursday College," developed several years ago at Monroe Community College in Rochester, New York typifies attention to the type of concerns cited in this section. Faculty members and student affairs staff, working together, identified the need to develop a special scheduling option to serve a specific population within the community—the adult female. A program was developed that provided these students with an opportunity to attend college two days a week, from 9:00 a.m. to 4:00 p.m., and study on a full-time basis. Considerable adjustments were made by faculty and student affairs staff. The program required a restructuring of procedures by admissions, registration, scheduling, financial aid, counseling, student activities, and the bursar's office, as well as by academic departments. A full-time admissions counselor was assigned to coordinate the project, and transition support was provided to students through the development of special seminars and peer support groups.

The Faculty/Staff Perspective. The second form of interdependence links the college and its faculty, administrators, and staff. The institution expects a certain level of productivity and involvement, and personnel expect appropriate remuneration and freedom to work in a pleasing environment. Beyond these elementary aspects of interdependence, however, is an array of interrelationships, expectations, and responsibilities that grows in complexity as rapidly as student populations change.

Faculty, staff, and administrators must be kept current with information affecting curriculum development, student needs, recruitment, funding sources, legislative compliance requirements, college procedures, research findings, academic governance activities, and the direction of the institution's strategic planning. Goals and objectives compatible with institutional mission must be clearly stated, attainable, and understood by all members of the college community. This can only occur when the institution maintains open lines of communication among all individuals. Through such open communication and the resultant feelings of "ownership" that will likely develop, community colleges will realize a reaffirmation that people support what they help create.

The barriers among academic, student, and administrative divisions of the institution must be removed through cooperative involvement in interdivisional planning and problem resolution. The variety of pressures affecting community college operations requires a smooth and uninterrupted flow of information that mandates a cessation of all aspects of departmental and/or divisional provincialism. Herein lies not only one of the greatest opportunities but also one of the greatest challenges facing leaders in the collegiate environment.

Here, student affairs staff must assume an active role. As Flynn (1986) pointed out, student affairs professionals must serve as change agents who maintain close working relationships with faculty and staff to assist them, both directly and indirectly, in the identification of specific needs; the development of program objectives; the provision of student outcome data and advisement services; and, most important, the recognition of need for cooperative and collaborative efforts to fulfill the institutional mission. Floyd and Weihe (1985) suggested that student personnel administrators must serve as "loving critics" who listen and are responsive to colleague input. At the same time, they must assume a strong voice as the institution's educational conscience. Where change or innovation in educational programs and service are needed, they must convince faculty and staff that existing practices are inadequate and assure them that the proposed changes merit personal commitment. Cooperative effort is the key element in this process.

The dilemma facing student affairs leadership in this perspective on interdependence centers about the means to establish such collaboration and overcome "turf problems" without risking a loss of identify. It has been noted in recent years that several community colleges have attempted to improve internal collaboration by merging their Academic Affairs and Student Affairs Divisions. While this approach may offer the opportunity to provide central leadership and coordination for enrollment management, there is a risk of reducing the quality of student affairs and student development programming by narrowing the holistic or interdisciplinary approach of student affairs units to the more intradisciplinary perspectives of academic departments. It may be more appropriate to retain current administrative structures while enhancing cooperation between student affairs and academic affairs personnel.

An example of this approach can be noted in the Collin County Community College District (established in 1985) in McKinney, Texas. Although the college is in its infancy, professional staff have made decisions that will affect the fabric of this new institution. The decisions emphasize the importance of interdependent relationships as the norm and minimize barriers among faculty, student affairs staff, and students. Rather than hiring a team of counselors for a traditional counseling center, for example, leaders have decided to build programs on faculty advising with "student development specialist" support through in-service assistance and consultation. Faculty loads and contracts include specific reference to advising and follow-up with students. Student affairs professionals serve as generalists deployed in academic divisions and in a Life Planning Center (LPC). The LPC replaces several traditional student service offices and focuses on holistic development of students, from the point of entry to the college to their exit or transfer or entry to the workplace. Rather than coming to an admissions office, prospective students secure information and assistance through the LPC. Career development materials, advising support, job placement support, and transfer support are integral components of the LPC. Thus, elements of internal interdependence are maintained without loss of identify or diminution of service by any of the individuals or divisions involved.

Most community colleges, of course, are not in a position to reorganize along the lines of the Collin County program. As a result, community colleges must look to other means to develop a college-wide understanding of the benefits possible from the recognition and fostering of internal interdependence. Ironically, the external pressure of federal compliance requirements and the need for retention improvement have provided the impetus for greater internal interdependence. Student affairs staff in community colleges have, of necessity, become deeply involved in providing information, assistance, and programs that cut across traditional areas of functional responsibility in the collegiate environment. Most notable are activities related to the compliance requirements of such legislation as the Family Educational Rights & Privacy Act of 1974, Section 504 (Handicapped) Regulations and, most recently, the Standards of Progress Requirements for PELL grants. The increasing number of cooperative efforts in student advisement, course scheduling, and curriculum review for the purpose of retention improvement also suggest that such issue-related activity will provide the best means to illustrate the benefits of internal interdependence.

The Community Perspective. The community part of community colleges includes all segments of the society existing within the geographic area served by the institution. Since the individuals within that society were considered under the student perspective section, this discussion will deal only with societal groups or classifications with which community colleges are perceived to be most interdependent: educational institutions, business and industry, governmental agencies, and community organizations.

This may be the most controversial area of community college interdependence. Community colleges have been charged with attempting to be all things to all people. Ironically, it is also in this area that most community colleges have expended the least of their resources, for they have tended to delegate responsibility primarily to relatively underbudgeted community service, evening division, and extension site operations.

Educational institutions in the community are recognized as obvious interdependent connections. Historically, admissions personnel relied on their contacts with secondary school guidance counselors as primary sources for freshman enrollment. Four-year colleges and universities were courted both for their respect as peers (Cosand, 1979), and for their recognition and accreditation of transfer credit from the community colleges. Unfortunately, the type of recognition sought from four-year institutions was often denied to the secondary schools by many community colleges. Now, however, with predicted declines in high school graduates, these relationships are changing.

Community colleges are beginning to hear and to respond

to the criticism that there is insufficient articulation with secondary schools. As Cohen asserted (1983, p. 165), community colleges may have been "facing the wrong way." Ties need to be strengthened with secondary schools, and there are growing reports of the expansion of advanced placement courses and the development of better articulation agreements with secondary schools. Concurrently, four-year institutions are demonstrating new interest in, and acceptance of, relatively liberal articulation agreements with community colleges. The values of interdependence are being recognized at all educational levels.

Certain implications for community college personnel are clear. Community colleges must resist isolation and develop an understanding of the philosophy, objectives, and problems of other types of institutions (Cosand, 1979, p. 43). At the same time, personnel in other institutions must be made aware of the mission, goals, and efforts of community colleges. Rather than compete for students, funds, and programs, cooperative scheduling and programming efforts might be developed to enable all the educational institutions to use their respective resources more efficiently and effectively. There is an advantage to all through collaborative effort.

The need for the involvement of community college student affairs professionals in this area is critical. They must use their contacts with colleagues in both the secondary schools and the four-year institutions of higher education to facilitate the process. The positive effects of such activity in secondary schools have been noted in New York State, for example, through the development of two consortia involving community colleges with the local school districts and/or boards of cooperative educational services (State University of New York, Special Report, 1984). These efforts have been lauded for their quality, comprehensiveness, efficiency, and minimal cost. A prime example of cooperative effort with four-year institutions, through the efforts of student affairs staff, is in evidence at Monroe Community College (MCC), in Rochester, New York. Twenty-four different four-year institutions entered into agreements with the college that guarantee the acceptance of MCC graduates. A number of "2 + 2" arrangements have been developed with both public and private colleges that allow students to apply for simultaneous admission and guaranteed transfer upon completion of an associate degree.

Business and industry have several obvious interdependent relationships with community colleges, including the employment of community college graduates and the provision of tuition assistance for employees. A rapidly expanding form of collaboration involves the development by community colleges of contract courses to meet specific employer needs. Beyond these basic aspects of alliance, however, Hodgkinson (1983) suggested numerous other opportunities for the development of a true partnership. For example, barter possibilities may exist in the form of facilities use, faculty consultation and/or temporary employment, service on advisory committees and as adjunct faculty, tax write-offs for equipment donations, out-placement counseling programs for employees facing layoffs, shared research efforts and, of course, internships and cooperative education programs.

All of these efforts require an in-depth understanding by college personnel of the organizational mission, structure, operations, facilities, and procedures of local business and industry. Vocational opportunities, needed job skills, trends in employment, and other career planning information must be known by student development specialists. Conversely, student affairs administrators must be sure to acquaint business leaders, personnel managers, and training directors with all aspects of their college's resources and strengths. Quality of effort and service must be assured and maintained.

It is in this area of community interdependence that student affairs professionals can find exciting opportunities. Activities that range from facilitating tours of industrial and research installations as part of staff development programs to the creation and implementation of special developmental services for industrial personnel will become apparent to innovative staff. A wide range of special opportunities is available for creative student affairs professionals.

Shook (1983) described the Career Assessment Center at Austin Community College as one designed to match training needs of individuals with the needs of area employers and to provide programs for experiential credit. In Omaha, Nebraska, the Metropolitan Technical Community College collaborated with Northwestern Bell Telephone Company to develop a retraining assistance program for craft workers (Floyd and Weihe, 1985). Community college career counselors worked directly with the employees to develop new career directions and to adapt to the changing requirements of the labor market. Similarly, through a direct contract with one of its local industries, Monroe Community College (New York) developed a "Career and Educational Assessment Project" (Flynn, 1986). Academic and student affairs officers worked closely with industrial representatives who expressed need for an out-placement program to assist their employees facing layoff. The program permitted the industrial employees an opportunity to work directly with qualified counselors at the college and to receive an assessment of their career and educational goals and opportunities. As a result, the college not only provided a service, but also developed additional FTEs for a specific population that otherwise might never have looked to the college for assistance.

These are examples of the many possibilities that exist for development through the alliance or interdependence of community colleges with business and industry. The fact that such alliances also enhance community colleges' images of quality and prestige is evidenced by the comments of New York's Lieutenant Governor, Alfred B. DelBello (SUNY Special Report, 1984): "The talents and the technical know-how of our community college faculty members, shared so effectively in our contact courses with industry program, give New York an incalculable edge in the national and international marketplace" (p. 16).

Governmental agencies and community colleges are interdependent primarily in areas related to financial support and legislative compliance. The colleges look to county, state, and federal governments for direct support, special program grants, and/or tuition assistance for their students. The agencies, in turn, demand accountability and compliance with procedures, policies, regulations, and laws. Beyond these basic relationships, however, lie an array of interdependent affiliations with specific governmental offices, departments, and service agencies.

Most community college student affairs professionals have had extensive experience with some aspect of this area of interdependence. In fact, due to the interrelatedness with funding, this is probably the most overworked area. Consider, for example, job training and/or retraining programs (e.g., Job Training Partnership Act and Office of Vocational Rehabilitation), the Veterans Administration, Social Security, Armed Forces recruitment personnel, and the morass of paperwork related to financial aid validation and certification.

Again opportunities are ripe for innovative student affairs professionals in this area of interdependence. It is argued by some, in fact, that if they had been observed and responded to earlier, community colleges would not be continually struggling to ward off the encroachment of governmental control on their internal operations. The key here, as Cosand (1979) pointed out, is communication and the "educational job" to be done with public officials so that each community college ". . . is viewed externally as a cohesive institution committed to quality education for the total community" (p. 34).

The many varied methods to develop this communication may include invitations to public officials to serve as speakers, panel members, moderators, or respondents on programs related to public issues; requests for public officials to serve as visiting lecturers in courses offered by the departments of political science, criminal justice, and human services; consistent recommendations of academically superior students for participation in county, state, and federal legislative intern programs; the development of innovative means to enable public officials to have the benefit of feedback from a microcosm of the constituents they represent; and, of course, the development of special courses and programs to help resolve the major social, economic, and environmental concerns within the community.

To benefit from the opportunities provided through interdependent relationships with governmental agencies, community colleges must stay current with legislative actions and grant opportunities as they develop. If a college is not sufficiently large enough to have a development officer or grant specialist for whom this is a primary area of responsibility, then student affairs professionals may step in to fill at least a portion of the void. Through contacts with their colleagues at other institutions, professional associations, legislative reports, and regular reading of news media in the field of higher education, innovative professionals can develop an immediate programmatic responsiveness that will be beneficial to both their community and their college.

Community organizations may not be perceived as interdependent with community colleges in that there is seldom direct contact, an exchange of funds or services, or even, in many cases, a mutual understanding of respective missions. As a result, this may be a potentially fruitful area for development and expansion of interdependent relationships. Included in this area are a wide variety of civic organizations, art groups, preservation societies, service organizations, philanthropic groups, not-for-profit organizations, business and professional associations, social organizations, church groups, and self-help or special interest groups. Numerous opportunities exist with these organizations for assistance with the development of their program. A prime example of such activities took place several years ago at Monroe Community College in New York. A church adjacent to the college campus was exploring opportunities and means to raise funds through the use of their church school building during the week. At the same time, students and student affairs professionals at the college were exploring the possibility for developing a day-care center on campus. Through cooperative efforts, these interests were successfully united and a not-for-profit day care program was established in the church facility. The success of this venture has been of benefit to the college, the church, the students, and all other members of the community who participate in the day care program.

An overview of the community perspective reveals some interesting parallels between the community college and adult education movements. This seems to be especially true in the areas of student affairs and counseling services. Phoenix (1970) indicated that the challenge facing evening student affairs workers in the 1970s was one of revising the institutional image not only among students, but also among the faculty, staff, and general public. Since evening college clientele consisted of adults who, in one way or another, were active in the community, he suggested that the colleges must continually attempt to meet community needs in order to be vital for them and, further, that student affairs administrators need continually to evaluate and present community needs to the faculty for their consideration. Finally, he noted that it was most often the student affairs worker who is closer to the pulse of the community than any other individual on the college faculty or staff.

These concepts must now be recognized as integral to the philosophy of all student affairs workers in the field of community college education. Many organizational structures have changed in accordance with changes in student characteristics and community needs. Operational practices and institutional missions have been adjusted to incorporate many of the activities formerly relegated solely to adult education and community service departments. Student affairs workers, within the limitations of time and budgetary constraints, must respond accordingly by extending the scope of the community they serve to include all the areas defined in this chapter.

The Challenges of Interdependence for Leadership in Student Affairs

As stated earlier, the primary interdependence in colleges is between the institution and its students. Heretofore, with few exceptions, the foundation for this interdependence has been centered around the full-time student. In fact, since a majority of funding was generated by the full-time student, the institution concentrated its efforts on building strong support services primarily to meet their needs. Currently, however, a new interdependence is forming as the shift to more part-time students takes place. Advice from Helfot offered in Chapter 2 is pertinent in this interdependent context as well.

The implications are clear. The nontraditional student may well become the new traditional student. Colleges and universities, therefore, will have to change not only the way that they recruit, counsel, and advise, but also change course offerings and the availability of services and programs to meet student needs. Extending advice for leaders given in the preceding chapter, this discussion will focus on specific professional activities related to interdependency.

Some may argue that sound programs for the part-time or the adult student are currently being offered. While this may be true, it is doubtful that many institutions have developed strong support services to the breadth and extent necessary to serve the needs of this increasing population. Both a shift in institutional resources and a change in philosophy will be necessary.

Student affairs professionals may be in the best position to serve as change agents on campus, assisting in the development of programs and services to attract and serve the new mix of community college students. Therefore, the primary challenge for student affairs staff is to shift from an interdependence that, in the past, was primarily relegated to the traditional student, to one of interdependence with the total community served by the community college. Few individuals on the community college campus will have the opportunity to learn and convey the breadth of information at the community college as will the student affairs officer. The student affairs professional should become, to the extent possible, an active partner in many classroom activities. For example, accounting and chemistry are two courses that have extremely high attrition rates at most community colleges. Such is the case even with students who have just completed high school and are familiar with the rigors of study. What about returning adults who may not have been in the classroom for many years? What chance of success will they have in such courses unless there are specially developed services to assist them in returning to the educational mainstream? Qualified counselors can work in conjunction with faculty to provide assistance for such special students.

In addition to the expanded scope, there is a change in the nature of the interdependence with the student body as more older students attend community colleges. Recent high school graduates may require less recognition for their life experience than older students, who expect more of the institution than the mere recitation of facts, figures, and philosophy. The adults will be more demanding to know where their program of study will take them. Many of them will have life experiences to call on; thus, the level and quality of interdependence between the institution and its students will increase, as it should.

Over the years, it has consistently been the student affairs staff who have advocated for students and interpreted student needs to the faculty and the administration. At no time has the change in student mix been as dramatic as today. As colleges must now vigorously recruit many of these part-time students (as well as full-time students) to maintain funding, student affairs officers may be asked to provide the necessary leadership.

References

Cohen, A. M. (1983). Leading the educational program. In G. B. Vaughn & Associates, *Issues for Community College Leaders in a New Era* (pp. 159-185). San Francisco: Jossey-Bass.

Cosand, J. P. (1979). Perspective: Community colleges in the 1980's. *Horizons Issues Monograph Series.* Washington, DC: American Association of Community and Junior Colleges, Council of Universities and Colleges and ERIC Clearinghouse for Junior Colleges.

Cross, K. P. (1981). *Adults as learners: Increasing participation and facilitating learning.* San Francisco: Jossey-Bass.

Floyd, D. L., & Weihe, L. S. (1985). Commitments to non-credit students: Issues for student development educators. *Journal of Staff, Program, and Organization Development.* 3(4), 128-132.

Flynn, R. T. (1986). The emerging role for community college student affairs personnel. *NASPA Journal, 24*(1), 36-42.

Hodgkinson, H. L. (1983). Establishing alliances with business and industry. In G. B. Vaughan & Associates, *Issues for Community College Leaders in a New Era* (pp. 222-231). San Francisco: Jossey-Bass.

Knight, B., & Orozco, K. (1983). Learner recruitment case study: Triton College. In J. Roueche & E. Baker (Eds.), *Beacons for Change: An Innovative Outcome Model for Community Colleges.* Iowa City, IA: The ACT National Center for the Advancement of Educational Practices.

Kuh, G. D. (1981). *Indices of quality in the undergraduate experience* (AAHE-ERIC/Higher Education Research Report No. 4).

Washington, DC: American Association for Higher Education.

Lindquist, J. (1981). Professional development. In A. W. Chickering & Associates, *The Modern American College* pp. 730-747). San Francisco: Jossey-Bass.

O'Banion, T. (1971). New directions in community college student personnel programs. *Student Personnel Series of the American College Personnel Association, No. 15.*

Phoenix, E. W. (1970). The challenges of evening college student personnel services. *Journal of Student Personnel Work in Adult and Evening Education*, 4(1), 9-16.

Shook, G. (1983). Assessment of local industry, business, and government training programs for credit. In D. L. Floyd (Ed.) *Catalyst Exchange Community Services Catalyst*, (13)2, Blacksburg, VA: National Council on Community Services and Continuing Education.

SUNY Special Report. (1984). *The community colleges on the move.* Albany, NY: State University of New York.

Vaughan, G. B. (1983). Introduction: Community colleges in perspective. In G. B. Vaughan & Associates, *Issues for Community College Leaders in a New Era* (pp. 1-20). San Francisco: Jossey-Bass.

Chapter 4

Opportunities in Challenge

John Cordova, Kay Martens

Current reports on the quality of higher education emphasize student involvement as an important condition for excellence. Student services programs can play a significant role in student involvement. In the community college, the diversity of the student population and certain unique institutional characteristics present special challenges. As Helfgot suggested in Chapter 2, the student population is characterized by patterns of interrupted involvement, work, and home priorities that compete for time and attention and often by undefined goals and weak academic skills. Increases in part-time faculty, declining resources, unclear missions, and conflicting priorities also affect programs. The need to address these challenges has led to a national concern on the part of student affairs professionals, and the process of clarifying purposes and functions has begun.

A number of the challenges unique to community college student services are identified in this chapter. Ideas for coping with the challenges and ways of increasing student involvement in learning are suggested. Both the challenges and the development of new ideas create opportunities for leadership at the college and national level.

Challenges with Students

A major challenge is provided by the nature of the student of the two-year college. Helfgot, in Chapter 2, portrayed the students as diverse in attendance patterns, reasons for attending college, and interests in other life tasks while attending college. These qualities of students and the conditions in the colleges they engender likely will continue, according to Cross (1985), who recently emphasized that all segments of higher education "will be serving a far wider spectrum of the population on every dimension—more women, more ethnic minorities, more people from low income brackets, more part-time students, more commuting students, more older students, more underprepared students" (p.22). Two-year colleges also serve recent high school graduates, veterans, employees upgrading job skills, concurrently enrolled high school students, and honor students. A major consequence of the condition of serving students of such a variety of backgrounds and personal qualities is that it makes it difficult to focus professional attention on *typical* developmental needs.

Many of these students also enter the institution with underdeveloped academic skills and, thus, create another special challenge for student affairs professionals who must respond to a need for strengthening basic skills. Astin (1985) documented and decried the decline in academic preparation of entering college students. Hodgkinson (1985) predicted that the number of college students who need academic assistance will increase. Roueche (1985) and Moore (1976) noted that community colleges have always confronted the challenge of the academically underprepared student.

Astin's (1985) summary of student survey results indicated changes in the educational and career plans of students. "Students' increased interest in business and other high-paying professional careers has been accompanied by increasing materialism and greater concern for attaining personal power and status" (p. xv). According to Astin's research, the goal to be financially well off was identified by 70% of the students. Thus, an increase in pragmatism on the part of students has led to a decrease in interest in participating in any college activities not directly related to career or job goals. College student affairs professionals need to respond by encouraging balance in educational programs.

Paradoxically, the decrease in interest in the liberal arts and in people-related professions is occurring at the same time as are shifts to a technological society that will emphasize an individual's skills both in learning how to learn and in interpersonal behavior. Students will need basic skills, according to Cross (1985), as "the tools for lifelong learning" (p.12), and the ability to synthesize and to apply information. Chickering (1982) identified cognitive and affective skills important for success at work and highlighted the importance of interpersonal skills: communications skills and "accurate empathy . . . defined as both the diagnosis of a human concern (based on what a person says or how he or she behaves) and as an appropriate response to the needs of the person . . ." (p.5). Presumably, student affairs professionals understand the importance of these skills. The challenge is to involve students in activities that will help them to acquire and to appreciate interpersonal skills.

Unfortunately, some students limit their involvement in classes. Roueche (1985) focused on the importance of students' involvement with their studies by declaring time-on-task as the most important factor in student learning. Yet his research, and that of others, illustrated that many community college students are minimally involved in their academic work, often regarding it as a minor part of their already very busy lives. For example, the typical community college student identified by Richardson, Fisk, and Okum (1983) was the requirement meeter—the student doing just enough to pass required courses.

Minimal involvement in college activities is, of course, exacerbated by part-time attendance. Sixty-four percent of all community college students in 1984 were enrolled part-time. Cohen and Brawer (1982) noted that fewer students than in the past are completing two years of study—less than one in five in 1980—and that many discontinue enrollment after their first year. Two-year college students sample courses available in the curriculum and attend intermittently. Cohen and Brawer (1982) suggest that "this pattern of *ad hoc* attendance seems to fit the desires expressed and demonstrated by students who are using the colleges for their own purposes" (p. 58). While this pattern of attendance may respond to some needs of students, it makes it very difficult for student affairs professionals to *intervene* in any important way to promote development uniquely attributable to the college experience.

Part-time enrollment and commuting, rather than living on campus, are circumstances that tend to make the learning experience parallel, but essentially external, to students' lives (NIE, 1984). Lack of residential living opportunities may preclude students from taking advantage of many out-of-class socialization opportunities, such as common study groups, extracurricular activities, and mentoring from residential hall advisors. For residence students, the opportunities for involvement range from general socializing to more personal exchanges involving such activities as helping, sharing, studying together, and working on projects (Pace, 1982).

There is a positive correlation between students' satisfaction with college and living on campus versus living off campus. Unfortunately, as Chickering (1974) noted: ". . . there are no significant responses to the special backgrounds of many commuting students, no attempts to deal with the difficulties they have in discovering and connecting with academic programs and extracurricular activities suitable to them, and no solutions to the difficulties they face in building new relationships with students and faculty members and with the institution itself" (p. 2). Two-year college student affairs professionals are no more able to respond to these conditions than professionals in other commuter institutions.

Without such programs and activities, commuter students are less likely to be involved, and the institution will be hard-pressed to say that opportunities for total student development were provided. A major challenge for student affairs staff is to develop programs that would broaden the college experience for commuting students.

Concern with student involvement is reflective of a larger concern with the quality of higher education. In a recent National Institute of Education Study (Study Group on Conditions of Excellence . . ., 1984), student involvement was identified as "perhaps the most important" condition for excellence. "There is now a good deal of research evidence to suggest that the more time and effort students invest in the learning process and the more intensely they engage in their own education, the greater will be their growth and achievements, their satisfaction with their educational experiences, and their persistence in college, and the more likely they are to continue their learning" (p. 17). Similarly, Astin (1985) stated that ". . . the effectiveness of any educational policy or practice in developing student talent is directly related to the capacity of the policy or practice to increase student involvement" (p. xiv).

Challenges for the Institution

A number of institutional characteristics work against the community college as a promoter of student development. Increasing use of part-time faculty, changing or unclear institutional goals, and declining resources are challenges that need to be considered by student affairs professionals.

The higher the proportion of part-time faculty, the more difficult it becomes to maintain collegiality, to assure continuity in the instructional program, and to preserve coherence in the curriculum (Study Group on Conditions of Excellence . . ., 1984). The proportion of faculty who teach part-time is now over half— 56% in 1980 (Cohen & Brawer, 1982). In some institutions, these figures are even higher. In Illinois for example, in 1970, 52% of the faculty were part-time. By 1974, it had increased to 63%. The part-time faculty in Florida increased to 78% between 1970 and 1974. Of 34,300 California faculty in 1975, there were 14,273 full-time and 20,027 part-time. These numbers refer only to part-time faculty with no other institutional responsibilities (Cohen & Brawer, 1977).

One of the essential elements of a student affairs program is that everyone in the institution has a role to perform to promote student development, including faculty. A chief criticism of the use of part-time faculty is that they are neither required to, nor are they rewarded for, assisting students outside of class. In most instances, office space is not even available for part-time faculty. According to Cohen & Brawer (1977), ". . . the part-timers tend not to be evaluated as full-timers, do not participate in faculty development, have little contact with students outside class, and have practically no contact with their peers" (p. 58).

Perhaps more distressing is the difficulty part-time faculty have in identifying with the goals of the institution and thereby becoming involved with the institution. Without the opportunity to interact with their full-time teaching peers, there are few, if any, possibilities to share ideas about how to promote student development. If two-year colleges are serious about encouraging student development, opportunities must be provided for part-time faculty to interact with students, peers, and administrators. Innovative programs for part-time faculty need to be developed so that they can broaden the college experience not only for students but also for themselves. Perhaps what is needed most to enable progress in this area is an institutional reward system that recognizes the obligation to work with students in and out of class.

Faced with declining enrollments and resources, governing boards and presidents have had to wrestle with the problem of evaluating the overall mission of the institution. The concept of "sticking to the knitting" (Peters & Waterman, 1982) has begun to be applied by some. In two-year colleges, the "knitting" is thought to be excellent teaching and guidance of students. Attempting to be all things to all people, community colleges often are found in an identity crisis (Gleazer, 1971) exacerbated by differing perceptions of the mission as viewed by various constituencies, such as legislators, board members, and registered voters (Richardson, Doucette, & Armenta, 1982).

In 1974, O'Banion stated that ". . . the identity crisis of the community junior college stems from unclear priorities rather than from any lack of distinguishing characteristics" (p. 13). "Mission blur" results from attempting to accomplish many priorities, to be all things to all people. One of the challenges, and opportunities, for student affairs personnel is to increase institutional awareness of the importance of student development goals to the mission of the college.

The lack of clarity about mission leads to difficulty in establishing institutional priorities, which in turn creates confusion for staff who ask, "What is this place supposed to be doing and what am I doing in it?" (Cohen & Brawer, 1977, p.40). Unfortunately this confusion often creates conflicting institutional practices. One example of such a conflict is the difficulty in reconciling services designed to provide easy access to college with those established to properly place entering students. The community college has developed a reputation for providing easy access to college. With improved technology, it has become even easier to register by telephone and through the mail. These procedures improve access to the college but may result in students enrolling in courses without proper advisement or placement assistance. It is often feared that assessment programs will create barriers to easy access provided by telephone registration and affect the number of students entering college.

In the past decade, concern has increased over the need to address the basic skill deficiencies of a growing number of students. Many colleges and some states have adopted mandatory assessment, advisement, and if indicated, placement in remedial courses. The emphasis of these programs is on improving the quality of instruction and increasing student retention. Paradoxically, these programs are often implemented on the same campuses that are establishing telephone registration.

Another quality versus quantity paradox created by unclear priorities is often seen as a conflict between liberal arts and career education. There has been a concerted national movement to reinstate the importance of the liberal arts and sciences by strengthening general education requirements. This is sometimes perceived as creating additional time requirements for students whose intent is to complete a few courses or to concentrate on an occupational curriculum. These paradoxes provide a challenge to student development personnel to assist the institution in developing quality programs without having an impact on the quantity of students attending the college.

One of the foremost challenges to community colleges is the reality of declining resources. The era of rapid growth during the 1960s and the 1970s has ended for most colleges. Several states have passed tax-limitation laws that are designed to limit the growth of governmental expenditures and/or set ceilings on property tax rates (Cohen & Brawer, 1982). Developing creative solutions to this challenge is a universal problem. As Breneman and Nelson (1981) indicate, "More than any other sector of higher education, community colleges face a fluid future, with important choices to be made regarding which programs to stress and which people to serve. Questions of financing policy, therefore, quickly become entangled in broader questions of educational purpose and priorities" (p. viii). Viewing this problem optimistically, community colleges now have an opportunity to look differently at what must be done.

Student affairs staff can do little to change declining resources. However, many of the institutional challenges in implementing student development programs relate to questions or concerns about the mission of the college. In assisting to clarify the mission and to develop priorities, student affairs staff have the opportunity to increase awareness of the importance of student development.

Challenges for Student Affairs Staff

As community colleges are encouraged to change to accommodate changing clientele, student affairs staff also are asked to reexamine their role and function within the institution. Local reexamination by student affairs personnel, governing boards, and presidents has now moved to the national level.

For example, in 1981, the Dallas Community College District began a review of its program. A semester-length study of the student services functions was conducted, and several seminars were offered throughout the district to heighten the awareness and involvement of student affairs staff and others. In 1982, a Statement of Student Services Philosophy and Purposes was issued. From this statement, goals and implications for action were developed. The report indicated the following: "In many cases, the philosophy, purposes, and goals represent a continuation of current practices. But our directions are clarified, crystallized, and emphasized by these statements. Too often, our efforts have been fragmented and disjointed because the common purposes toward which we were working were unstated" (DCCCD, 1983).

In 1983, The Maricopa County Community College District established a District Task Force on Student Services to review and analyze its programs and recommend changes for the future. A series of hearings were conducted with 32 groups of employees throughout the district, including faculty, student affairs personnel, staff, and administrators. The first report on the findings is being prepared and will be revised by the task force. By early Spring 1986, a district-wide discussion will have been conducted to review and revise the report's recommendations, which will subsequently be submitted to the chancellor. Dallas and Maricopa provide two examples; other community colleges have conducted similar reviews of their student services programs.

One of the many challenges student affairs personnel face is the question of who is responsible for student development. It is difficult enough to determine what role faculty and student affairs personnel should assume. A review of literature indicates that there is disagreement among student affairs staff as to which service areas should be responsible for student development. An assumption the authors make is that student development is the responsibility of all community college personnel. A major responsibility of student affairs personnel, faculty, and administrators is to initiate and develop programs in which the educational focus of the college community is on contributing to student growth and development in a unified and coherent manner (Cordova, 1983).

A study by Cordova (1983) of community college faculty, student affairs workers, counselors, and administrators identified each group's perceptions of responsibility for student development. The respondents also were asked to indicate who actually assists students to acquire specific life tasks. The results of the study indicated that there were significant differences among and between groups' perceptions regarding who should be responsible. All groups perceived counselors as being most responsible and administrators least responsible (Cordova, 1983). It is interesting to note that student affairs workers (counselors excluded) perceived themselves as being less responsible than faculty for assisting students to evaluate their development.

On the question of who is actually involved in assisting students to acquire specific life skills, there were also significant differences in perceptions. All respondent groups perceived administrators as being least involved in assisting students. Counselors perceived themselves as being more involved than faculty, but faculty perceived themselves as being almost equally involved as counselors in assisting students. Administrators and student affairs workers did not perceive any group as being significantly more involved.

The results of this study are consistent with the concerns of Lloyd-Jones and Smith (1954), Mueller (1961), and Harrington (1974) about the separation of the student affairs function from the instructional program. "This schism has perpetuated a difficulty for student personnel workers in perceiving themselves as educators" (Harrington, 1974, p. 14). Ten years later, the Traverse City Statement (1984) stresses the same idea: "The student development professional is an essential and integral member of the community of educators, which is responsible for creating and maintaining learning environments, providing programs and services, and integrating these educational experiences to meet the life-skill needs of students and staff" (p. 3).

The challenge for student affairs staff is to provide leadership in redesigning student services, exploring new approaches for integrating student development with instruction, and involving all college personnel in the achievement of development goals.

As discussed in the first section of this chapter, the concern for increasing student involvement relates to the national concern with improving the quality of higher education. Involvement is defined as ". . . how much time, energy, and effort students devote to the learning process" (NIE, 1984, p. 17). Students who are involved in the learning process, within as well as outside of the classroom, interact with faculty, student groups, and often work on campus. By contrast, uninvolved students show some of the characteristics of part-time and commuting students; they have minimal contact with other students and often experience academic difficulties.

Research by the American College Testing Program (Noel, 1976) demonstrated that students' involvement in the institution—persistence with advisors, in student clubs and organizations, in work-study jobs—is linked to retention. While student involvement, like student retention, is a college-wide responsibility, it is often the student affairs professional who provides the leadership for designing and implementing college activities to promote student persistence.

Lindquist (cited in Astin, 1985) recognized that four-year commuter colleges, like community colleges, have special problems involving students in the institution. He suggested four steps to generate greater involvement among students that are also applicable to two-year institutions: (a) engage in brainstorming sessions with administrators, student affairs staff, library staff, and certain community counterparts to discuss ways to work together in creating a rich environment for higher learning where commuters live; (b) make administrative schedules flexible to accommodate the diverse schedules of commuters; (c) seek community and commuter experience in the staffing of the institution to generate a stronger capacity to empathize with commuters, and be sure that staff members whose only experience has been in residential colleges are thoroughly acquainted with the specialized needs of commuters; and (d) conduct faculty development activities focusing on the diverse learning objectives, backgrounds, styles, and special interests of commuter students, then help teachers redesign their courses to fit commuter profiles (Astin, 1985, p. 190).

A key factor in involving part-time and commuting students in college is recognizing that their time is limited and that college is only one of their many priorities (NIE, 1984). It is important to help students understand the time demands of college as part of their initial orientation and advisement process. The example that Roueche (1985) cited of a new student who was planning to enroll full-time while working and raising a family is not uncommon. It highlights a major advisement need—helping entering students make realistic decisions. Chickering (1974) suggested "developing an admission and orientation center that provides preadmission information and assistance and that helps students clarify why they are coming to college, what they want to do, and how they will do it through initial orientation workshops and through such additional follow-up activities as are required for particular individuals with special problems" (p. 134).

Student services is recognized as a critical component of efforts to increase student involvement. The study group for Excellence in Higher Education (NIE, 1984) recommended that "all colleges should offer a systematic program of guidance and advisement that involves students from matriculation through graduation. Student affairs personnel, peer counselors, faculty, and administrators should all participate in this system on a continuing basis" (p. 31). However, "a major problem is that student services programs have rarely been integrated within the mainstream activities in community colleges" (Deegan, 1984, p. 14).

A key aspect of this integration is close coordination between student affairs personnel and instructional faculty. For example, Astin (1985) refers to academic advisement as "one of the weakest areas in the entire range of student services" (p. 165). However, academic advisement is more often the responsibility of instructional faculty than of student affairs personnel. As such, it should be planned jointly, with faculty training student affairs personnel on curriculum requirements. Student affairs staff could help faculty develop good advising techniques, including career planning, interpersonal skills, and listening skills. Participating in advisement can help all members of the college community familiarize themselves with all college programs.

These and other ideas for increasing student involvement require institutional support. As recommended by NIE (1984): "Academic and student service administrators should provide adequate fiscal support, space, and recognition to existing co-curricular programs and activities for purposes of maximizing student involvement. Every attempt should be made to include part-time and commuter students in these programs and activities" (p. 35).

Challenges for Leadership

In the preceding section, a number of examples were provided that can strengthen the student affairs program in the community college. These are exciting ideas and programs, but they are not new. Thus, the major opportunity for leadership is not the development of ideas and programs; rather, it is understanding and moving beyond the roadblocks to implementing student development goals in the community college.

The National Council on Student Development of the American Association of Community and Junior Colleges convened a national colloquium on "The Vitality and Future of Student Development Services in Two-Year Colleges" at Traverse City, Michigan in August, 1984. From that colloquium came the recommendation that ". . . student development professionals need to re-examine their program priorities, their roles within their colleges, and the future direction of their profession" (p. 1).

The League for Innovation in Community Colleges initiated a national project "to develop a new statement on student development for the latter part of the 80s that will hopefully provide direction well into the 1990s" (O'Banion, 1985). The 1960s provided a maintenance model for student services. In the middle of the 1970s, the human development model began to emerge. Now in the middle 80s, there is again a need to provide another model, according to O'Banion. There is some disagreement among student affairs professionals and community college leaders as to what is the best model or models for providing effective and integrative student services. However, there is agreement on one point. As Elsner and Ames (1982) state, ". . . student services need to be redesigned. The student services function needs an infusion of new ideas, new approaches, and a new reason for being" (p. 139).

O'Banion (1985) articulated one of the leadership problems: "Like a ten-year locust, the need to develop a contemporary statement on the role of student development in the community college burrows its way to the forefront of the national education agenda once again" (p. 1). It is difficult to remain excited about defining concepts that were defined in the 1960s. It is hard to list, as was done for the Traverse City Statement (1984), strategies and recommendations that have not been listed before. This does not mean that it is not important, that it does not need to be done, or that new ideas are not possible. However, it is important to recognize that redefining concepts over and over may constitute a block to responsiveness to current conditions.

There are other obstacles to implementing student development goals on a community college campus. They vary by institution according to the leadership provided by the chief student affairs officer; the president's understanding and support of student development; the background and interests of student affairs personnel, faculty, and staff; the resources available, and other factors. Some impediments include the following: (a) lack of institutional planning and/or lack of involvement of student affairs personnel in institutional planning; (b) expecting student affairs leadership but not establishing hiring criteria related to the profession or providing in-service training; (c) assuming that student development costs more or that additional staff have to be added to do it rather than redesigning existing programs; (d) discouraging staff from trying new things by not acknowledging innovation, even if it doesn't work perfectly; and (e) assuming that increased enrollment is the only criteria for evaluation or by not defining criteria for effective programs. Each of these impediments needs to be addressed through creative, but professionally sound, leadership. Leadership requires insight into the real problems of the two-year college, integrity to deal with the problems honestly and forthrightly, and the knowledge to design effective programs.

Some student affairs leaders are reexamining roles and functions to better serve a changing student clientele within changing institutional constraints as has been cited in this chapter. Changes in roles and functions generate opportunities for leadership. They also generate opportunities for university preparation programs and national associations to work with community college personnel to develop ideas that can be incorporated into training programs.

Examples of the leadership needed from professional associations include the Traverse City colloquium and the cooperative efforts of various student affairs associations on the Council for the Advancement of Student Service/Development Program. Regional workshops, such as those provided by Commission XI of the American College Personnel Association, are also useful in providing affordable opportunities for practitioners to discuss program ideas. In addition, training programs focusing on specific concepts and skills would be valuable.

Compared with four-year colleges and universities, the

community college faces certain unique challenges in implementing student development goals. However, these challenges also provide unique opportunities for new leadership from student affairs personnel and for creative programs that can result in new opportunities for students.

References

Astin, A. W. (1985). *Achieving educational excellence.* San Francisco: Jossey-Bass.
Breneman, D. W., & Nelson, S. C. (1981). *Financing community colleges: An economic perspective.* Washington, DC: The Brookings Institution.
Chickering, A. W. (1974). *Commuting versus resident students: Overcoming the educational inequities of living off campus.* San Francisco: Jossey-Bass.
Chickering, A. W. (1982). Liberal education and success at work. *Center for the Study of Higher Education Bulletin,* College of Education, Memphis State University, 5, 3-6.
Cohen, A. M., & Brawer, F. B. (1977). *The two-year college instructor today.* New York: Praeger.
Cohen, A. M., & Brawer, F. B. (1982). *The American community college.* San Francisco: Jossey-Bass.
Cordova, J. A. (1983). *Perceptions of community college personnel about student development.* Doctoral dissertation, Arizona State University.
Cross, K. P. (1985, September). *Education for the year 2000.* Paper presented at the meeting of the Arizona Women's Partnership, Phoenix and Tucson.
Dallas County Community College District Student Services Staff. (1981-1983). *Emerging directions: Student development in the DCCCD.* Dallas: Unpublished report prepared by the VPSS Council.
Deegan, W. L. (1984, May). The alternatives: Revitalizing student services program. *Community and Junior College Journal,* 14-17.

Elsner, P., & Ames, W. C. (1983). Redirecting Student Services. In G. B. Vaughan, & Associates (Eds.), *Issues for community college leaders in a new era* (pp. 139-158). San Francisco: Jossey-Bass.

Gleazer, E. J., Jr. (1971). The emerging role of the community junior college. *Peabody Journal of Education, XLVIII*(4), 255-256.

Harrington, T. F. (1974). *Student personnel work in urban colleges.* New York: Intext.

Hodgkinson, H. L. (1985). *All one system: Demographics of education—kindergarten through graduate school.* Washington, DC: Institute for Educational Leadership.

Lloyd-Jones, E., & Smith, M. R. (Eds.). (1954). *Student personnel work as deeper teaching.* New York: Harper and Brothers.

Moore, W., Jr. (1976). *Community college response to the high-risk student: A critical reappraisal.* Washington, DC: American Association of Community and Junior Colleges.

Mueller, K. H. (1961). *Student personnel work in higher education.* Boston: Houghton Mifflin.

Noel, L. (1976). College student retention—a campus-wide responsibility. *The National Association of College Admissions Counselors Journal, 21*(1), 33-36.

O'Banion, T. (1974). *Teachers for tomorrow: Staff development in the community-junior college.* Tucson: The University of Arizona Press.

O'Banion, T. (1985, August). *A national statement on student development programs in community colleges: Here we go again!* Unpublished manuscript.

Pace, C. R. (1982). *Achievement and quality of student effort.* Unpublished report prepared for The National Commission on Excellence in Education. (US Department of Education No. ED 227-101).

Peters, T. J., & Waterman, R. H., Jr. (1982). *In search of excellence.* New York: Harper and Row.

Richardson, R. C., Jr., Doucette, D. S., & Armenta, R. R. (1982). *Missions of Arizona community colleges: A research description.* Tempe: Arizona State University, Department of Higher and Adult Education, College of Education.

Richardson, R. C., Jr., Fisk, E. C., & Okun, M. A. (1983). *Literacy in the open-access college.* San Francisco: Jossey-Bass.

Roueche, J. E. (1985, November). *Excellence in developmental education.* Speech presented at the Maricopa Community College Developmental Education Conference, Phoenix, AZ.

Study Group on the Conditions of Excellence in American Higher Education. (1984). *Involvement in learning: Realizing the potential of American higher education.* (National Institute of Education Publication No. 246 833). Washington, DC: US Government Printing Office.

The National Council on Student Development of the American Association of Community and Junior Colleges. (1984, August). *The vitality and future of student development services in two-year colleges.* Unpublished paper presented at Traverse City, MI colloquium.

Chapter 5

Opportunities in the Future

Don G. Creamer

A clear and compelling picture of certain problems evident in the current condition of two-year colleges has been painted by Dassance, Helfgot, Phoenix, Flynn, and Floyd, and Cordova and Martens in earlier chapters of this monograph. The vividness of the picture seizes the imagination and enlivens the conscience of student affairs professionals. Yet these thoughtful analysts skillfully draw attention in their painting to the opportunities for student and faculty achievement accorded by the special nature of the two-year community college. Like acknowledging the centrality of light, color, shade, or object in a great painting, a viewer of this scene painted by the authors of the preceding chapters can recognize the overriding issue or theme of the authors' comment: A unique assessment of reality is the cornerstone of vision.

From a rich heritage of general educational service to expanding and changing markets of students, the two-year college has an uneven record of commitment to and accomplishments of student affairs programs. Dassance chronicled this record in Chapter 1, effectively setting the stage for the discussions about student diversity and interdependence of educational programs of the two-year college in Chapters 2 and 3. Cordova and Martens focused attention of practitioners on the paradoxical, side by side existence of problems of the colleges and challenges to professionals in student affairs in Chapter 4. Each discussion included recommendations for leadership.

One of the realities of practicing student affairs professionals in two-year community colleges is that conventional or normative behaviors may not be good enough or may not be the correct behaviors. This unpleasant fact is true both for the present and for the future and must be faced as a prerequisite to planning for change. A foundation for effective practice cannot be made of faulty building materials and, even if only a suspicion of fault exists, it should not be trusted. Though the point can be made more dramatically in the example of construction of nuclear power plants, the bottom line in higher education is not terribly different: People may suffer from poorly designed or constructed delivery systems of a vital commodity. Is education less vital to the realization of human potential than energy?

The counterbalancing reality of student affairs practice in the two-year community college, also sketched by authors of the preceding chapters, is that the special nature of the institutional type is rich in heritage and in potential. The two-year college embraces egalitarian goals compatible with national public policy and has carved its niche in the American way of life because it delivers on a promise. Americans believe in the land of opportunity promise embedded in political history; yet without the two-year college system, opportunity in higher education would not be shared equitably across this nation. People of all manner and character come to learn by experiencing educational programs often not available at other types of colleges. They are taught by professionals sometimes near missionary in their enthusiasm for their work. No less important, they are taught by other students, sharing the goal of opportunity made possible by attending a two-year college.

Given this assessment of reality of two-year college potential for promoting student development, a vision of opportunity in the future can be formulated. Four elements of that vision will be outlined in the sections to follow, grounded in the substance of Chapters 1 through 4 but raised to a level of synthesis and made generalizable to planning for the future. **Characteristics of a potent learning environment** will be outlined first, followed by **a standard of organization effectiveness, a profile of a new student affairs leader**, and, finally, as has been the theme of this monograph, **certain challenges to the leadership** of the profession will be issued.

Characteristics of a Potent Learning Environment

The goals of a college cannot be met until the goals of its students and faculty are met (Astin, 1985). The goals of a college are embodied in student and faculty aspiration and are represented by the organization in the public mind. Thus, an environment created by the organization/faculty/student interaction may be judged by the degree to which it encourages and enables individual goal attainment.

It is normal or common to think of student goals in a context of the college experience, at least to the extent that students come to college to learn. What they wish to learn may be stated in the language of personal goals. "I want to improve my earning capacity," "I want to learn new skills," and "I need credentials for my chosen career" are typical goals for students in college.

Some nudging by thoughtful educators is sometimes required to remember that faculty seek personal improvement as do students and that the organization is encumbered by these aspirations just as surely as by student goals. Astin (1985), for example, calls for a talent development model as the preferred standard for judging excellence in higher education. It is not solely the resources acquired by the institution, nor its reputation, focus of the curriculum, or achievements of its graduates that determines excellence, according to Astin's argument. The central determinant of excellence should be the degree to which student *and* faculty achieve their goals within the context of available talent. Outcomes for students and faculty should be judged in perspective of inputs: How much talent was developed with the raw materials or human potential available?

Thus, the first characteristic of a potent learning environment is **student and faculty achieve their goals**. Students achieve their goals by willingly submitting to a process intended to change them. Through information acquisition, reflection and study, interaction with faculty and students, and experience of life and work, they acquire new knowledge, attitudes, values, beliefs, and behaviors. Faculty achieve their goals by productivity on the job; through a search for greater knowledge, wisdom, or skill; and by setting and achieving personal goals for life.

A central feature of the environment is goal setting and effort. Everyone in such an environment recognizes the advantage of learning or changing and is devoted to the quest. It is not selfish that faculty should seek self-improvement when their job responsibilities call for promoting student improvement; it is a prerequisite. Only by constant growth can one qualify as a facilitator of growth in others.

The centrality of goal setting in such an environment must be secured by organization policy and professional effort. The formal fabric of the organization must recognize this feature in written and spoken forms. Its policies, procedures, job description, and evaluation and reward systems must acknowledge the responsibility of all to set goals for themselves and to teach others to do so. When teachers teach, counselors counsel, and administrators administer, they must remember that effort follows clear direction. It seems more likely that one will arrive at a designated place, either in life or in geography, when the place is known beforehand.

Effort is the offspring of goals. Though it often occurs naturally, the organization again must formally recognize the corollary by structuring its curriculum and all other educational programs to require effort. While some learning may occur passively, most does not. All students and all faculty should be encouraged to be active participants in the learning process.

Activity in a learning environment spearheads the second characteristic of potency: **The environment is interactive**. Almost all forms of development occur as a consequence of interactions with the environment. It is in this manner that individuals recognize other forms of reasoning or values that attract them and that energize them to seek new understanding and new patterns of living.

Student/faculty interaction must be managed for potency. Organization leaders can and must shape the norms and culture of faculty and students. A conscious decision is required to so organize, structure, integrate, and differentiate reporting and authority systems to necessitate constant and meaningful interaction. For example, college leaders may elect to define academic advising as a process of paper shuffling associated with registration, or they may prefer a definition that approximates academic advising to individualized teaching or even mentoring. By dozens of these conscious choices, educational leaders can enhance the potency of the learning environment.

What is the product of such interaction? Meaningful interactions produce accurate knowledge of self and, if properly conducted, create a climate of free choice. The third characteristic of environmental potency, then, is that **valid information is generated and free choice as to its use is encouraged**. This characteristic is central to interventionist theory (Argyris, 1970), which holds that lasting change, either within the normative culture of an organization or within its formal structure, is enhanced by such democratic values.

Setting goals, perhaps through significant interaction with others, is more likely to stimulate effort to achieve them when accurate information both about self and about the goal is generated for self-enlightenment. An intentional product of academic advising, for example, might be knowledge of self, of careers, and of values. It may be reasoned that such empirical information will be used out of rational self-interest. It thus becomes a most potent tool for education: Help people generate knowledge about and for themselves in real world contexts, and they will use it and will change.

Standard of Organization Effectiveness

Working to enhance environmental potency must be anchored by some standard that signals success or failure. What is the expected or desired outcome of goal-directedness through interaction? A reasonable set of standards can be derived from this perspective and can be expressed thusly: A two-year community college is effective to the extent that its students grow intellectually, enhance personal values, improve self-esteem, acquire or refine skills, and express satisfaction; that its faculty grow in productivity, personal goal attainment, and expressions of satisfaction; and that the organization promotes a potent learning environment, is responsive to needs, and is efficient. This view of community college effectiveness is influenced by Cameron (1981), whose research shows a critical relationship of variables such as those proposed in this standard to effectiveness in other types of organizations. The adaptations to the two-year college setting are shaped by concerns indigenous to the institutional type and to a developmental perspective of education.

Evidence of student growth should center on the intellectual forms of development. At the base of all development is knowledge of self and of one's world, perspective gained from cognitive growth, and an enhanced ability to act based on reasoning and meaning. All segments of the community college should focus on promoting intellectual growth, not only because it is central to the historic nature of higher learning, but also because it may act as a prerequisite to other personal, social, or psychological forms of growth. Promoting intellectual development comes first—for student affairs professionals and for all other educators—and forms a basis for promoting the development of the ". . . individual as a whole" (ACE, 1937), the well-rounded person.

The enhancement of personal values is often a direct consequence of interaction with others and is a natural by-product of the potent environment described above, as is improved self-esteem. Students learn new skills under the tutelage of wise faculty, and they practice them within the diverse environment shaped, in part, by faculty interest, knowledge, and skills.

Expressions of student satisfaction, never adequate as a single indicator of effect, should be used as a capstone in the area of effects on students. The form of the request for satisfaction comment by students should be expressed in a context of student goals: Were you satisfied with your goals and the manner in which the organization enhanced your achievements? In this manner, the focus is on the effects on the individual, not merely on pleasing aspects of relationships or activities.

Faculty growth should be evidenced by enhanced productivity (Are faculty able to do more or to do better that which is required or which is chosen?) and by empowerment to achieve personal goals (Are faculty growing as human beings in knowledge, wisdom, and skill?). This domain of organizational strength may then be capped—as with the student domain—by expressions of satisfaction.

Domains of effectiveness for the organization should focus on the potency issue first. Is the organization structured to promote development? Is the environment interactive? Does the environment promote the generation of data about its members?

A second aspect of the overall organization judged to be critically related to its ability to achieve its mission is its capability for responsiveness. Community colleges thrive on responding to community need for educational programs. How well does the organization identify and interpret needs for education? At what costs to other programs can the organization quickly add new efforts? Responsiveness—held universally in the two-year college world to be an institutional virtue—may hide an organization cancer, an unstable pattern of commitment to central values of higher learning. When anything that can be called education or training by someone in the community is routinely packaged for delivery by the two-year college, it is virtually inevitable that an institutional identity crisis is forthcoming. Whether responsiveness contributes to organization effectiveness is a judgment that should be made ethically as well as philosophically.

The organization also must be efficient for it is the steward of resources provided in trust to deliver on promises. Efficiency need not be equated to a profit motive. The issue is morality: Did the organization make the most of its resources?

A Profile of a Future Student Affairs Leader

The student affairs leader of the future shares direct responsibility for the realization of a potent learning environment and for clear understanding of domains of organization effectiveness. The accomplishment of these feats requires extensive knowledge not commonly associated with student affairs professionals and the possession of expert skills in administration equally foreign to the profession. The leader must

be knowledgeable of historic student services, of development of adolescents and adults, and of organization development,

be a researcher or a "data-oriented journalist" about students, faculty, and the organization,

be a systems analyst, a strategic planner, a developmental programmer, an organization effectiveness specialist, and a teacher,

value the goals of general education,

be a skillful communicator, and

have vision.

The times that allowed administrators to practice holding the simple credential of "liking to work with people" are gone forever (if the practice was ever adequate). The times that allowed administrators to practice by picking good people, then allowing them to do their jobs, may be destined for a short life. The student affairs leader of the future will probably enjoy working closely with colleagues and students and will certainly be an adept judge of professional ability, but the leader will also be an active educator in the most demanding sense of the term.

The knowledge required of the new leader is vast. The history of higher education and student services' role in that history may serve as a cornerstone; then, knowledge of development—both of students and of the organization—must adorn the foundation and provide the basis for day-to-day operations and planning. The leader must be able to provide guidance to other professionals in student affairs, to teachers, and to administrative colleagues grounded in accumulated theory, research, and literature. This person may be a risk taker but will be wise enough not to waste human potential by trial and error strategies.

No administrative tool is more potent than data that accurately represent or describe reality. Planning should be data-based, as should administrative decisions, and the student affairs leader of the future should take the initiative to collect data about students, faculty, instructional and other educational programs, and the institution and disseminate them to potential users. The need and the task may be seen as an ongoing story to be told by a journalist-in-residence—one driven by a search for the truth and a compulsion to share it.

What data should be generated by the student affairs leader? The need for data about students and about faculty has been established and is concerned with forming a basis for goal setting. The data associated with the student, faculty, and organizational story is more descriptive and normative in nature. For example, the following questions might guide the collection of certain data:

Do students of similar ability perform equally well across curriculums?

Do students requiring financial assistance achieve comparably with those who do not?

Which student services can be shown to have a direct effect on student persistence?

Other than earning credits, what general effects on student development are directly associated with attendance at the college?

What do students say about their college experience?

To what extent have personal needs of the professional staff been met within the employment context?

Do grading practices promote student achievement?

Does the application of certain institutional procedures, such as those in admission, advising, and reporting of student progress, have the desired effect on students?

Are institutional values applied consistently to all students?

Obviously this list of questions is incomplete and may not even include the most important questions within specific institutions. Perhaps, however, it can be seen as representative of the nature of the stories that need to be told. They should be told honestly, and they should help institutional leaders answer the moral question posed earlier: Has the maximum been achieved with the raw materials available? (Is the college the best that it can be?)

The student affairs leader of the future *must* be a researcher—perhaps much like the investigative reporter—who demonstrates concern for the enterprise by exposing its true nature for all to see and understand. The old excuse—"I am too busy to conduct research"—must be discarded; new challenges—"There are stories about the college that need to be told"—must be accepted.

Another cluster of competencies required of the new leader includes systems analysis, strategic planning, developmental programming, organization effectiveness monitoring, and teaching. If these competencies appear to go beyond traditional boundaries for student affairs, that is as it should be. The student affairs leader of the future must be involved meaningfully with the management of the entire institution, and to do so the new leader must possess executive-level competencies. A dean or a vice-president meaningfully engaged in the activities inherent in the exercise of these competencies might be said to be functioning as the president's right hand, sharing or anticipating the chief executive's requirements for effective institutional management. That is precisely where the student affairs leader of the future must function—at the president's right hand.

The nature of these duties may be discerned from a growing body of suggestive literature (Barr, Keating & Associates, 1985; Cameron, 1981; Chickering, 1981; Delworth & Hanson, 1981; Kuh, 1985; Sandeen, 1982; Smith, 1982; Strange, 1981; Winston, Miller, Ender, & Grites, 1984). These authors hold their own views about the future of student affairs, but they share certain beliefs and ideas that overlap the discussion of competencies. Each set of competencies serves to affect overall institutional effectiveness in its own way; yet they are interrelated. The thread that ties the competencies together is an institutional view of educational impact. The new leader must see the whole picture much as the president must see it, then stand ready to act as one sees the target and knows how to hit it. Likely the president cannot be involved in every administrative initiative of the college, nor can the chief student affairs officer, but the latter can, and must, be directly involved in most institution-wide initiatives.

The competency of teaching deserves special description in this context. It means to impart knowledge in a very direct way just as it means in any other context; however, in this sense, it also means the primary duty of leadership. The leader of the future must be constantly alert that the role of dean or vice president never becomes the end of leadership. **The end is development in students and the means is teaching.** The leader must teach in all duties, leaving as secondary concerns the accomplishment of administrivia (even though it may seem very important at the moment). Going about the work of teaching is the goal of the new leader.

The new leader will be involved in many aspects of the institution heretofore left to others, and that fact demands firm footing within the heritage of higher education. Most teachers are guided by their disciplinary viewpoints; their discipline provides a lens to examine reality. Thus higher education always honors diversity and balance of viewpoints on all issues because there are many disciplines, each with its own methods and perspectives on truth. Similar to disciplinarians, the student affairs leader of the future must be rooted in the heritage of higher education. As it always has been, the liberal arts—or perhaps general education—is the home of student affairs. The aims of the liberal arts and the aims of college student affairs work are almost synonymous, even to the language used to communicate them. The student affairs leader's view of higher education will be given direction and consistency by publicly recognizing the historic footing of applied behavioral science in the liberal arts. Whether it is a recognition of development as the aim of education or the primacy of democratic values in all that we do, it is the tradition of liberal arts that explains the essential character of student affairs professionals. A leader must honor this reality.

Finally, the new leader must have vision. A view of a better world should guide all actions of the new leader for, without it, leadership is hollow and perfunctory. Vision is a necessary, if not sufficient, ingredient of leadership for the future.

The Challenge of Leadership

Helfgot made clear in Chapter 2 that two-year college students may not resemble the collegiate stereotype. Even if the students are 18 to 21 years of age, the opportunities to behave according to the stereotype are limited in most two-year colleges. A possible generalization from his portrait of students is that they resemble a cross-section of American society. Does this condition suggest substantially different needs of these students in an educational context? Probably not. But it does indicate substantially different response modes from student personnel professionals. Older adults may use available services in unconventional ways, and they may hold higher expectations from professionals than younger students. They will likely obey the same laws of nature regarding a constant search for identity or a never-ending quest for more adequate powers of reasoning, but the fabric of their experience is more complex and the consequences of inadequate resolution of developmental tasks more poignant. They require better professional service than is conventionally provided in most two-year colleges. It is as simple and as complex as that.

The overriding challenge of leadership, therefore, is to provide better professional service. It must be better than what is now provided in two-year colleges, and it must be better than what will be minimally required in the future for any college. The demands for professional service are greater than in other colleges; the environmental circumstances that shape the quality of deliverable service are more adverse to conventional practice than in other colleges. But the simple truth remains: Quality education through student affairs practices in the two-year college is achievable only by more adequate responses to student and organization need than is now available.

Where is the guidance for better service to be found? It is not available in the mainstream of professional practice. No aspect of higher education is more driven by norms and convention than is student affairs. It is not available from administrative colleagues. They tend to be driven by competition for resources and would likely prefer a reduction in student affairs practices to free resources for other uses. It is not available from educational leaders who head our professional associations or from appointed leaders in government. They have not the experience, training, or the will to tackle problems in a professional area not absolutely critical to institutional functioning.

Guidance for future practice is available, on the other hand, from our researchers, our historians, and our philosophers. Our researchers point to basic truths about institutionalized education, our historians provide perspective on timeless values, and our philosophers help us understand our world as it is and allow us to imagine a better world.

The challenge of leadership is to make accurate appraisals of all contingencies of education for student development, grasp as fully as possible the knowledge of our profession, and elevate planning for the future to an extension of principles grounded in these two perspectives. A brief discussion of three such principles is presented here to be illustrative of the challenge:

Education for student development is the aim of all professionals in higher education. The obvious corollary is that education for student development is not limited to the results of student affairs practice. All professional educators are in the same business. It follows, therefore, that it is not the primary job of student affairs to provide service to students not available from other educators; rather, it is the job of student affairs professionals to provide **precisely the same service** as other educators. Phoenix, Flynn, and Floyd might extend their argument presented in Chapter 3 and call for interdependency in professional responsibilities. Student affairs professionals can render this valuable service in at least two ways: (a) They can join with teaching and administrative colleagues as a team, or (b) They can teach for student development through specialized programs that extend the work of teaching and administrative colleagues in other contexts that would not otherwise be managed without student affairs staff involvement. The most important point to be made about the application of this principle is that the role of student affairs professionals is to teach.

The goals of education for student development are synonymous with the goals of liberal (or general) education. It follows then that the methods of the student affairs profession are extensions of the methods of liberal educators. It is consistent that student affairs educators see themselves as behavioral scientists who search for better or more accurate understanding of people. It is consistent that student affairs educators facilitate better understanding of self through studies of history, anthropology, literature, religion, economics, and similar disciplines. It is consistent that student affairs educators see their role as promoting intellectual development in students without excluding other forms of development. It is consistent that student affairs educators teach the values of education for life as Dewey did. Dassance saw this connection and described it in an historical context in Chapter 1.

Methods of practice should require principled behavior from professionals. Cordova and Martens identified several problems associated with two-year colleges that have a direct bearing on the practice of student affairs work. Two-year college students do not live in residence, for example. It follows that their experiences with college will likely not be as intense, and perhaps not of equal quality, as peers in other types of colleges. Principled behavior by student affairs professionals would compel them to address this problem. It may be argued that a failure to act to correct a recognizable inequity in educational service is immoral. The overriding need for professional response in this situation is to insure equitable (quality) education even if it means diverting attention from more conventional service-oriented needs. What might they do to correct this problem? Other principles and other contingencies must be considered in deciding precisely what response to make in this situation. Perhaps the answer is in a vastly redesigned academic advising system requiring very different forms of participation both of advisors and of students than is usually required. Perhaps the answer lies in reformation of the curriculum requiring more individualized projects, such as research into important areas of life.

There can be little doubt, based on the discussions in preceding chapters, of real and compelling challenges for leaders in two-year colleges. They may appear overwhelming; yet most important quests are difficult. The advice of authors in this treatise is to search constantly for enlightenment, make unwavering commitments to lasting values, and act on principle.

References

American Council on Education. (1937). *The student personnel point of view*. Washington, D.C.: American Council on Education.

Argyris, C. (1970). *Intervention theory and method*. Reading, MA: Addison-Wesley.

Astin, A. W. (1985). *Achieving educational excellence*. San Francisco: Jossey-Bass.

Barr, M. J., Keating, L. A., & Associates (1985). *Developing effective student services programs*. San Francisco: Jossey-Bass.

Cameron, K. (1981). *Domains of organization effectiveness in colleges and universities*. Reprint Series: Organizational Studies Program. Boulder, CO: National Center for Higher Education Management Systems.

Chickering, A. W. (1981). *The modern American college*. San Francisco: Jossey-Bass.

Delworth, U., & Hanson, G. (1981). *Student services*. San Francisco, CA: Jossey-Bass.

Kuh, G. D. (1985). What is extraordinary about ordinary student affairs organizations. *NASPA Journal, 23*(2), 31-43.

Sandeen, A. (1982). Student services in the '80's: A decade of decisions. *NASPA Journal, 19*(3), 2-9.

Smith, D. G. (1982). The next step beyond student development: Becoming partners within our institutions. *NASPA Journal, 19*(4), 53-62.

Strange, C. C. (1981). Organizational learners to student development. *NASPA Journal, 19*(1), 12-20.

Winston, R. B., Miller, T. K., Ender, S. C., Grites, T. J., & Associates. (1984). *Developmental Academic Advising*. San Francisco: Jossey-Bass.